WE'VE HAD THIS FIGHT BEFORE

A brief guide on why couples fight and what to do about it

**Claudia Grauf-Grounds, Ph.D.,
Licensed Marriage & Family Therapist**

We've Had This Fight Before:
A brief guide of why couples fight and what to do about it
Claudia Grauf-Grounds

Interior Design: Annie Mesaros
Cover Design: Rosie Gaynor
Illustrations: Suzi Spooner
Copyeditor: Madison Frambes

Published in the United States by Honors Press.
ISBN: 9780998753300

For contact information visit: https://drclaudiagg.com

contents

When you walk down life's path
with your eyes closed,
you are probably going to trip over
something hard.

If you keep your eyes open,
you can see where you want to go.

READ
this first

(seriously, read this)

Have you ever felt like you and your partner are fighting the same fight—triggered differently, maybe—but over and over?

Maybe you're among the couples who try to avoid these recurring conflicts. You might try to make some changes or not enter into "that topic" of conversation. You might find that when you speak really loudly about it, your partner won't go there either. You might even try to practice some communication skills that you have learned. Whatever your attempts, these fights often keep showing up. So what do you need to know to address these recurring fights so you can partner better?

Sometimes our our eyes are not quite open—we need to unpack, slow down and review our reactions.

SOME EXAMPLES OF COMMON TYPES OF FIGHTS:

Example 1 (Biology): Dating for about 6 months, Chris and Pat had met through mutual friends. Although both college educated and working in satisfying jobs, they had been attracted to each other for different reasons. Pat was responsible and attentive to Chris; Chris laughed openly and had a set of friends who welcomed Pat into their circle. But Chris was questioning the relationship. Pat commonly wanted to call it an evening early and was beginning to think Chris was flirting with others. A mostly unspoken tension began to develop between them.

Example 2 (Family/cultural legacies): Together for almost 4 years, Rebecca and Miguel had managed their busy jobs and home life quite effectively. But now things were different. Frequent fights emerged around money. Maybe it was due to Rebecca working part-time after their son Sammy had been born, but they had managed on less income before. Miguel got frustrated with Rebecca every time he opened their VISA bill to see a new purchase for the baby. Rebecca got defensive and started to justify to Miguel that their son needed the things she bought. They found themselves wondering if they had made a mistake about getting married.

Example 3 (Relational Pain): Rachel sat eyeing her cereal, playing with her banana slices in the bowl. Why had Brett come home so late? At least he could have sent a text. Were his friends more important than she was? She felt alone and neglected. When she mentioned something in passing to Brett, he got defensive and said there was nothing wrong with spending some time with his buddies and that she didn't like watching NASCAR anyway. Maybe she didn't have a right to be feeling this way.

The purpose of this book is to help you better understand your intimate relationship tensions and expand the ways you respond so you can connect more deeply with your partner. Human beings struggle to explain our difficult encounters as we attempt to make meaning in life. The good news: fights often repeat themselves in three predictable ways.

Not 300 fights but 3 fights repeated 100 times each.

The examples on the left page represent the three inherent differences and core struggles every couple faces as they move from being single to functioning as a couple. The specific content of a fight may change, but it often ends up in the same place. The three core conflicts stem from differences in our biology, our cultural/family backgrounds and the emotional longings we bring to our partner. We'll dive into the three core conflicts in the following chapters, but first let's review some myths couples in conflict often embrace.

Why I wrote this book

I want to help you understand and better identify the three core fights that couples have, matching each to the skills needed to address that particular fight. As a therapist and teacher of therapists, physicians and clergy, I want you to learn to fight wisely.

When couples partner well, they:
- live longer and healthier lives
- report happier and more satisfying relationships
- parent the next generation better
- contribute more effectively to society
- adapt to life crises better

But most importantly, intimate relationships satisfy a deep longing to be connected to something bigger. We can support another who can support us. We can experience how someone holds our best interests in their heart and mind. Yet, many couples struggle to be there for one another in this deep way. There are patterns to this disconnect and I want to help you recover or find your path to connection.

This book is written for the average couple—those just beginning their relationship and those in relationships that have gotten stuck in unproductive and unsatisfying patterns. This book may be useful for, but is not intended for, those in a crisis. I would suggest that those with more complex problems seek professional help.

When we feel left out or uncertain in our intimate relationship, the following questions commonly arise:
- Can this person meet my needs?
- Is this the type of person I want to be with?
- Will this person judge me?
- Am I going to be left alone since this person is pulling away?
- Is there enough love to go around or are we fighting for limited resources?

To address these questions, people often react to rather than reflect on what is going on. By reacting, we often provoke our partner to respond reactively as well—resulting in a viscious cycle of react-react. Remarkably, a couple can experience more intimacy as they pay attention to their patterns and find ways to get unstuck.

This book offers information and tools to help you better your relationship together. I won't ask you to stop fighting; I will warn you, that certain types of fighting styles are destructive. I won't offer simple answers; I will give you some basic skills to build a better relationship. I won't support the notion that you need to win; I will offer the hope that your relationship can win.

Remarkably, a couple can experience more intimacy as they pay attention to their patterns and find ways to get unstuck.

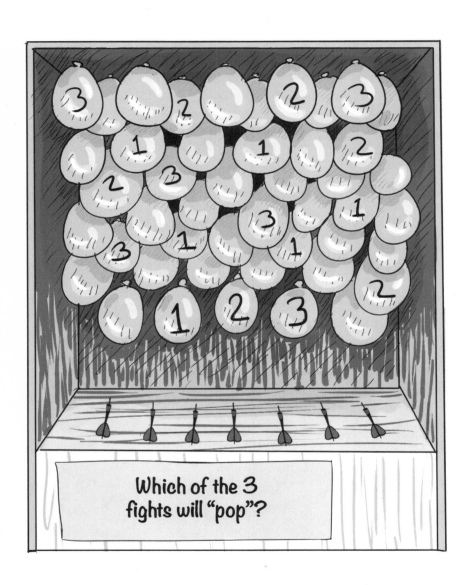

HOW TO
use this book

Conflict is normal because no two of us are the same—and the more life we share with each other, the more our differences become apparent. Some couples manage conflict unproductively. Family stress researchers point to two common reasons as to why people get stuck in negative interactions: ***beliefs*** and ***resources***. Beliefs refer to how you think about something. Resources are what or who you can bring into the situation to help.

Our society holds myths and expectations about relationships and conflict that are incorrect. For example, many people assume that loving couples won't fight or have arguments. The facts are clear: happy couples do have conflict, but they fight differently than unhappy couples. Since relationship myths contribute to the development of harmful patterns, we'll explore them in the next chapters, and give you some information to bust them. Then we will explore the three core fights in more depth. You are welcome to skip to the fight sections and return to the myth sections later.

beliefs + resources = coping

This book emphasizes **beliefs** first—how to make sense of the fights we have. I will review and break down the **three core flights common to most couples**.

Next, I will point to specific **resources** that may help with your particular type of fight. The **skills** you use will work more effectively if you match them to the core fight you are having.

Fight 1: Why can't you be more like me? *A-Skills*
Fight 2: Why can't you be more like my family? *B-Skills*
Fight 3: Why can't you understand my hurt? *C-Skills*

Therapists are often wonderful resources for couples when they get stuck in unhelpful interactions. *However, not all therapists are the same.* Some are better resources than others for your particular situation. The last chapter of the book discusses how you can help yourselves and also become better consumers of psychotherapy resources. It will save you money and time to pick a therapist who can work best with your particular couple fight pattern.

As someone who has trained others and provided couple's therapy for over 25 years, I have experienced the "good fit" and "poor fit" of therapy. This book will help you to determine some of these factors for yourself.

Overview of the next chapters

Let's revisit the premise of this chapter and this book: fights between partners are normal and found in predictable patterns. As people bring their whole selves—histories, cultures, and all—into close relationship, they will experience tension, overtly or covertly. This book will help you understand what's going on and show you what responses work best.

Throughout the book, you will notice numbers at the end of some sentences. These numbers correlate with the *References with Commentary* section at the end of the book. Research articles with expanded explanations can guide you to explore the ideas more fully.

Sometimes during a therapy session, after hearing the complaints and frustrations of each partner, I will pause and say, "So, it sounds like you two aren't married on this issue, yet." Couples that have been legally married for over a decade usually laugh out loud when I say this. They recognize that they are still fighting for the right to get their own way, as they did when they were single.

End-of-Chapter Exercises

After a description of each fight theme and the skills with which to address it, some chapters offer activities. Making observations and asking questions within your relationship can help to uncover what is going on. Becoming curious and learning from your partner may bring new opportunities for you to move forward together on the issues that concern you.

However, you must ask questions with an open attitude, sincerely willing to hear what your partner is able to tell you. (For those who practice mindfulness, this would fit well here). Sometimes people ask questions with a tone that indicates that they are really making a statement. Some people make observations when they are really trying to "prove" their point of view.

Genuine curiosity is respectful of the fact that each person in the relationship will have vital thoughts and feelings to share with the other. Curiosity makes space for new information in the relationship.

It takes TWO persons to work well on a relationship, but it only takes ONE to exit the relationship. You cannot fix another person, but you can learn to invite changes by being curious about your partner and by taking responsibility for your part. This book provides some ways to understand what might be going on for you. I hope this information may shift how you come alongside another.

Intimate relationships can be satisfying and meaningful parts of life. Like a plant that needs nurturing, relationships need attention and caring actions. Loving feelings are not enough to grow something that is healthy—we must work intentionally to improve our life together.

When I train family therapy graduate students, I have them participate in the following exercise to explore how couples might fight. You might try this with your partner.

Two students face each other each with arms outstretched, hands down. I ask them to stack their hands on top of each other, alternating each person's hand on top of their partner's. Then I say, "win," and I wait. The two almost always laugh and then they start "competing" to have their individual hand land on the top of the stack. I often hear faint cries of "ouch" as they feel the slap of the hand on top of theirs.

Now let's review the HOW of this fight. Usually, each individual experiences winning as being on top. Each is taking the "ME" position. Yet if we pull back and watch the interaction of the competition, we also see that when one person "wins" the other person "loses." Over time, the couple often pulls back from each other and the "relationship" loses—("ouch.")

I then ask my students to reflect for a moment and start over. Facing each other again with outstretched arms again, I ask if they might find another way to win. During this second exercise, the couple often holds out their hands side by side and then clasps their hands with one another. Each individual's hands and the relationship are noticed. When each recognizes the "WE," they also honor the "ME" and the "YOU."

"But I thought"

Fights and disappointed expectations.

MYTHS
about fighting

Many couples believe the myth that they are not supposed to fight. Some would say that fighting is destructive. And they have a point. When one person in a relationship wins consistently, the other partner and the relationship loses. However, to deal with fighting by taking a "don't fight" stance is not good advice. Not fighting in an intimate relationship is impossible, yes, impossible.

The belief that couples are not supposed to fight leads to denial or disappointment. Over time, the distance that grows between partners can lead to the death of the relationship.

Not fighting in an intimate relationship is impossible, yes, impossible.

Couples can learn to change their fights into constructive encounters. In the following chapters and as we explore the three fights, I will help you to connect your fights to the skills you need to make sure your fight is working for your relationship, rather than against it.

Before diving into the three fight themes that are active in most couple's relationships, let's explore a few key myths that get in the way. The next chapter provides even more myth-busting information for each of the following.

Myth 1:
Happy couples don't fight

Did you know that happy couples fight just about as much as unhappy couples?[1]

Does that surprise you?

Couples that stay together and those that move apart fight just about the same amount—but there's a difference. The difference is in the *quality* of what's going on **within** and **between each partner** during the fight.

Researchers and therapists can see, hear and measure these differences on several levels in each partner (e.g., blood pressure) and in the relationship (e.g., number of times the couple faces each other versus turns away).[2] I will explore this more in the Myth Buster section. Often, there are elements of *disappointed expectations* when these stressful situations occur. The three fight themes discussed in this book identify some central sources of each partner's expectations of each other.

Happy couples fight just about as much as unhappy couples

RELATIONSHIP STYLES

Validators | Generally calm and verbally responsive in communication and problem-solving; there may be some tension at times, but they can work through it and find common ground

Conventionals | Often take on gendered roles: women are responsible for relationship issues and the home, while men are responsible for financial support. Each person can initiate topics and make unilateral decision in their particular domain

Blamer-Placaters | One partner tends to point the finger to the problems in the other and that person generally accepts the blame and makes attempts to change

Avoiders | Partners rarely bring up issues directly; they may "blow up" at times, but then this is ignored. Each person internally feels frustrated and sometimes guilty. Often distractions are used when there is tension: drinking, TV or videogames, spending time apart

Over-Under Functioners | One partner experiences that they are taking on the main responsibility for the relationship to function; they work very hard in many life domains and believe there is unfairness and their partner could do much more

Devitalized | Both partners feel fairly hopeless about the relationship; they had tried in the past and had some success, but have mostly given up

Volatiles | Partners are reactive to each other when tensions rise; loud arguments and leaving each other in frustration are common in this pattern

Myth 2:
Most couples fight in similar ways

Fights can take many forms: many are subtle and not physical, loud, or verbal. Not all couples fight the same way.

One form of fighting is related to a couple's relationship style. Researchers name several common styles, including: Validators, Avoiders, Devitalized, Volatiles, Blamers-Placaters, Conventionals and Over-Under Functioners.[3] Therapists use these different styles to help the couple understand their particular difficulties. The list to the left defines some common Relationship Styles.

To really understand what is going on between two people, a couple's therapist or researcher needs to "read between the lines." The most important part of the fight often lies in the nonverbal communication and the interaction between the couple. Therapists call this "process."

The reason a therapist pays attention to process is because it is often this aspect of fighting that remains consistent over time. The content of the fight may change (e.g., being late or not helping with the dishes), but *the process takes on a similar form.*

Additionally, the particular process or "style" of the fight can undermine the relationship. For example, being an Avoider is a style of fighting that can build resentment in a relationship. In couple's therapy, I often use the image of a partner "sweeping the dirt under the rug." Over time, avoidance leads to a big lump growing under the rug that can easily trip either partner. Then a fight can become even more emotionally charged.

Myth 3:
Compromise is the most important couple skill in fighting

Sometimes compromise is a worthy skill to employ, but it can also lead to trouble in a relationship. *Many types of fights cannot be resolved well through compromise.* As you will learn later, only one of the three fight themes described in this book works well using the skill of compromise.

Let me give you a personal example. My husband can go for hours without eating and do just fine, but I can't. I'm hypoglycemic and need to eat every few hours or I get edgy or "hangry" (hungry+angry according to the *Urban Dictionary*)—my husband would call this something else. When we're out for a long day, the push and pull of our different "food needs" comes into play. Finding a compromise such as an "average eating time" does not resolve the problem. So what works? You will have to read the chapter on Fight #1 to find out...

Myth 4:
Communication skills help most couples

Many therapists help couples learn new communication skills. Most couples who seek counseling ask the therapist to help them with their communication. However, many basic communication skills work well only with certain types of couples.[4]

Much of the standard training in couple communication is based on training each partner to use a particular exchange of words. This practice can help the couple slow down, understand each other and negotiate more effectively. Although very useful at times, *this type of training misses out on much of what's going on.*

Sometimes the issue is not what you explicitly say. What could be more significant is the unspoken assumption beneath your words, through voice-tone or pulling away. And these communication skills may not fit your relationship style. When skills don't match the way the couple interacts, it is difficult to make lasting changes.

Sometimes the issue is not what you explicitly say.

MYTH
busters

So let's review each of the myths noted in the previous chapter and explore ways for you to understand your expectations about conflict more clearly.

The important thing is that you feel valued and are not alone in the interchange.

Myth Buster 1:

Embrace tension— it's normal

Myth 1: Happy Couples Don't Fight

Fights need to happen for your relationship to grow. They are vital. Just like muscles get developed only if they are taxed by exercise, couples that productively work through tensions will benefit. Couples can experience the rewards of a meaningful relationship in the midst of working through a challenge. In the long run, these encounters can increase the couple's sense of intimacy, understanding and even commitment to each other.

Sometimes a fight will require you to do something right away, but *many fights don't require an immediate solution.* In fact, many difficult interactions between couples are never fully resolved.[5] You don't have to resolve an issue to feel good or bad about the interaction you have had with your partner. The important thing is that you feel valued and are not alone in the interchange.

Fights indicate a developmental process necessary for two individuals to become one working unit. Each ME (each partner) brings in a set of beliefs and practices that are tied to their feelings, thinking, values and history. As a couple moves toward a WE (the couple working unit), there are bound to be differences and culture clashes.

In a sense, all couple relationships are cross-cultural experiences.

As the two cultures begin to merge and get closer, they will necessarily collide at times. These cultural collisions might fly under the radar or create a huge explosion. In either case, they usually result in tension between the couple. The tension can be soft or hard, with a mild amount of frustration between the partners or even "silences" that appear to pass quickly. Of course, sometimes a fight causes extreme pain and may lead to the couple questioning whether they will stay together.

> **In a sense, all couple relationships are cross-cultural experiences. As the two cultures begin to merge and get closer, they will necessarily collide at times.**

Myth Buster 2:
Fighting patterns vary from couple to couple

Myth 2: Most Couples Fight in Similar Ways

You can often trace fighting styles to early relationship interactions and early relationship stories that have "significance" for the couple. For example, one partner might believe it is best to "give in" to the wishes of her partner to show that she cares. She does not speak up about her preferences. Over time, one partner might "dominate" in the decision-making process. The couple does not expand to learn how to include what is important to both people.

Here's another very typical sequence for a couple. This pattern often gets a couple into trouble over time. P1 is one partner and P2 the other.

One type of Fight Style: Pursuer-Distancer

Look at the figure and begin with the top circle. Partner One reaches out to connect to Partner Two, but at that moment Partner Two looks away, emotionally pulls away and does not respond (maybe they are looking at their cell phone). Partner One criticizes Partner Two as "selfish" for looking away. Partner Two then responds by not reacting and becoming emotionally closed off (sometimes called stonewalling). As a result, Partner One feels more alone than when they reached out in the first place. This couple fight pattern can get stuck, repeated and creates damage over time.

So, go back and review some of the Relationship Styles listed under Myth 2 on page 20. Do any of these words strike you as describing what happens in your relationship when you fight or have tension with each other? You may want to show the list to your partner and ask them too.

A couple's fighting style, if stuck over time in a particular pattern, can predict whether the relationship will or won't work. Certain fight styles can also be associated with mental health issues like depression or can even make a partner more vulnerable to infidelity.[6]

Couples' research shows that non-verbal communication is a very powerful predictor of relationship break-ups. Even when one partner brings up a difficult topic and the other partner looks "calm" on the outside, a person's internal biology might evidence a whole host of physiological reactions, like increased heart rate and skin tension. The fight is showing up like crazy

Couples' research shows that non-verbal communication is a very powerful predictor of relationship break-ups.

on the research monitors, but the interaction will only show slight changes in the face such as a sneering smile or a raised eyebrow.[7]

Fights, no matter what style, have enormous potential to be redeeming and healing for the relationship. You can renew important learning and emotional intimacy in the context of "missing each other" and then coming together again. That's why make-up sex can be so great! Some researchers call these "repair attempts," and the ability to repair the relationship, once it has been strained, is central to couples who do well in their fight styles.[8] The good news is that you can learn some of these new response patterns. Just keep reading.

The good news is that you can learn some of these new response patterns.

Myth Buster 3:

The most important skill is moving between the ME, the YOU, and developing the WE.

Myth 3: Compromise is the Most Important Skill

Fights are interactional in nature. Things happen before, during and after a fight that lead to perpetuating or resolving the fight. The things that happen occur *inside each individual* as well as *between each person* and *within the larger relationship context*.

The domains are:
- *"identifying and sharing"* your own *concerns (the ME)*
- *"understanding"* what *your partner* is concerned about *(the YOU)*, and
- "finding" a way to *stay relationally connected (the WE)*.

The *ME*, the *YOU* and the *WE* are all included when you are skilled at effectively fighting as a couple.

In order to cope more effectively during a fight and work to resolve fights after they occur, a person needs to become like a wise prizefighter—assessing his/her own internal world, responding to their partner's "jabs" and finally panning back to scan the larger relational fighting context.[9]

Becoming aware of each of these positions is an essential aspect of effective fighting. The skill, then, is to learn to shift between these positions and not to get stuck in just one position. The couple can win a prize if they practice wise fighting strategies. The prize?: greater intimacy and connection.

Here's where it gets a little complicated.

Oftentimes, a person gets stuck in the **ME** position. *I* know how *I* feel, why *I* responded, what *I* was thinking. *I* am certain *my perspective* is the right one. What is fascinating is that you can lose the fight even if you are "right" about the point. That's because the HOW in the process of the fight is even ***more important*** and predictive of relationship outcome than the WHAT of the fight.

The WHAT of the fight is useful to understand (as we will explore in the fight theme chapters), but your RESPONSE to your partner is the most important factor. Constructive or destructive, you can find predictable and identifiable patterns.

Couples who fight effectively attend to all three domains and not just to the ME position.

The skill, then, is to learn to shift between these positions and not to get stuck in just one domain.

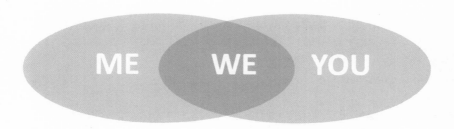

Wise Fighting: keep in mind the ME, YOU, and WE
in each context

Family systems thinkers call this commitment to the WE an example of second-order change.[10] It's like waking up from a dream and realizing there is another reality. This shift requires a new mind-set, new heart-set and new behaviors. Both you and those around you must "wake-up" to this new reality of the WE. A new system of relating to self and others is needed. In partnering, you have to wake-up to new ways of being, doing, feeling, and thinking.

Of course, many people try to stay asleep, in a sense. They attempt to recreate a younger way of relating because it's more comfortable and familiar for them. For example, one partner will demand their way (like a child's temper tantrum) and won't listen to what the other partner is concerned about. When a couple succeeds, they are waking-up to the WE. And some people are just not yet ready to wake up!

Commitment to the working unit of WE is key to achieving a successful relationship. However, you must lose or abandon the ME and the YOU components completely.

Good relationships require each person to make a transition from the ME to an awareness of the YOU and then a commitment to a new system, the WE. And the system needs to be new; the old cannot fit anymore.

Before we move on, I need to mention one other important factor: the larger context of the fight. The larger context in which the YOU, the ME and the WE operate will change and this will impact the fight too. In what arena are you fighting?

The foundational couple wake-up: Commitment to a NEW SYSTEM— THE WE.

Our relational encounters happen in the privacy of the bedroom, sometimes at the kitchen table eating with our family, sometimes on the phone within earshot of our co-workers or sometimes at an extended family gathering.

Each of these contexts will influence the kinds of information each partner is aware of and shares. The larger context may help the flow of information (e.g., relaxing on vacation at the beach), while at other times the larger context will inhibit what goes on (e.g., conversing about what kind of beer you want in front of your alcoholic brother at the family Thanksgiving gathering). Becoming aware of what contexts work for your relationship will help to shape how you manage your fight.

As you become aware of the opportunities or limits of a particular context for communication, you can make choices that work better for you as a couple—resulting in less victimization by your circumstances and more wisdom in your actions.

CULTURAL MESSAGES ABOUT THE ME AND THE YOU

When the ME wins consistently, the WE loses. Many messages within American culture value the ME over the YOU and the WE. From childhood, we hear that it is important to win, to be the best, to take top awards, to speak up for your rights, to do for yourself and to set boundaries. Competition is a central value in our work and in our leisure. It's not by chance that there is a term, "weekend warrior." We are coached in skills for our personal gain more often than in our interpersonal domains. Yet, healthy relationships require a sort of maturing in our sense of self to allow for the inclusion of the needs and concerns of another.

When the YOU wins constantly, the WE Loses. Not all cultural messages focus on the ME. You may be from a culture that attends to the needs of others as the priority over the individual ME. Messages about fitting in, being quiet and honoring others are much stronger than the messages about focusing on yourself. This cultural message might be particularly tied to gender messages too. Men are to be listened to more than women. Elders are to be obeyed and not questioned. Your needs are not important; it's the family needs that really count. Some cultures are more collectivistic, that is, the first priority is the survival of the community, while other cultures are more individualistic, that is, the needs of the individual must come first.

The point of this book is that ALL of the above domains, ME, YOU and WE must be attended to in order for an intimate partnership to thrive. When one of the three is "privileged" over the others, difficulties in the relationship, or to you as an individual, will emerge.

Myth Buster 4:
Skills need to fit the type of fight.

Myth 4: Communication Skills Help Most Couples

Most people try to avoid feeling helpless. Yet sometimes within our closest relationships, we don't understand what is going on. That's why people go to therapy. They don't go when things are running smoothly, they go when they get stuck. It often takes an outsider to help make sense of the things that are going on inside and between the two of you. Couples often seek to improve their communication skills when they go to a therapist.

Most therapists would coach a couple using verbal exchange strategies between the parties. The "classic" idea would be something like slowing down the conversation and having each partner explain...*"When you did that, I felt...."* and *"What I heard you saying was...."*[11] Although this practice can be very useful, many couple interactions are heated with emotion and are loaded with layers of information. Simplifying an exchange to this type of skill often feels dismissive of the complexity that is going on.

Some Hints of Things to Come

You may ask: "If basic communication skills don't work, what will work?" Let me offer some hints that we'll develop in the next chapters.

For some fights, you will need to stop, listen, and become more empathic. These exchanges are often communicated though touch and facial expression more than words. Thus, basic verbal communication skills would be inadequate to address many of the tensions that occur between partners.

For some fights, we need to change internally and challenge our expectations. These fights require each person to understand and accept that **both people** will have legitimate needs at times. These needs will be different and sometimes even competing with each other. Each person is unique and will function better when certain activities happen and will not function well if they don't. The skill of compromise, even discovered through the practice of good listening, may not be enough for this kind of fight.

The Potential Gift of Fighting

Fights are complex. There are many components that come into play: our behaviors, our expectations, and our histories including cultural and family beliefs. Invisible physiological and neurological processes take place as well. And I am talking about your brain— your brain in love. Sexual and emotional intimacy connects the primitive and reflective parts of the brain, so true change can't involve just one component.

You can't change behaviors by new thinking alone and you can't change feelings by changing behaviors alone. Your feelings and your body and your brain are involved in all of it. There is a complex exchange between these parts of yourself and these parts of your partner.[12]

Within the brain, neurobiological connections help to make new interactions possible and our primitive self-protector, the role of the brain's amygdala and limbic systems, are often tied up in these processes.[12] For example, when you feel threatened, your brain sends signals to your body to fight, to freeze, or to flee. These are very strong emotional components at work. When a relationship is more secure, we experience less threat; however, when we are in conflict, our emotional and biological protective signals will be triggered often.

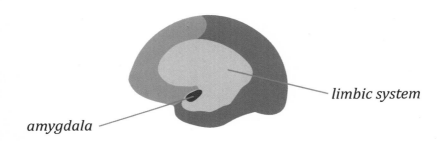

amygdala   limbic system

The potential gift for a couple and for each person in the relationship comes when safety and flexibility abound. This involves a couple's ability to attend to their differing needs within a safe and committed relationship. However, as soon as someone feels threatened or doesn't know what to do, all the primitive biological and protective systems send warning signals throughout the body and the brain, which impacts the ways we interact with another. That's when matching the fight to the right skills will be helpful.

The potential gift comes when safety and flexibility abound.

INITIAL EXERCISES

1. Select the Relationship Style listed on page 20 that best fits your relationship. Discuss why you picked this style with your partner; ask them to select and discuss one too.

2. The ME, YOU, WE Discovery Exercise
Over the next several days, reflect on and evaluate times when there is tension between you and your partner. Place a check mark under the ME Position if during the tension you could identify what you were personally concerned about. Place a check mark under the YOU Position if you could describe what your partner was concerned about during the exchange. Finally, place a check mark under the WE Position if you were able to "step back" for a moment during or soon after the encounter and say something like: "we need to work on how to do this together," or "we're not working as a team on this, let's figure out if we can be a team."

	ME Position	YOU (Partner) Position	WE Position
Tension Example			
Tension Example			
Tension Example			

3. Begin to Identify a "Fight Sequence"

Write down a recent "fight" or "tension" with your partner. Try to recall and write down what was going on before the fight. Then write down how you responded (include words and actions). Next write down how your partner responded to the fight (words, actions). Try to recall what was going on inside you (physically, emotionally, relationally). You might want to ask your partner the same things. If this fight has been resolved, how did that happen?

"Come play in the water!"

"Come stay on the beach!"

FIGHT #1

"Why can't you be more like me?"
or Different Biology

You Did Not Marry Your Clone

Biology is central to fighting. As a couples therapist, I often have one partner turn to me in the midst of a tense therapy session and say to me, "I just don't get it!" to which I respond, "Wonderful insight... that's SO true!"

In the amazing way we "fall for another," each partner is commonly drawn to a person who evidences "a difference" that complements him or her. It's true—opposites do attract! Emotionally reserved persons are drawn to those who are emotionally expressive or a more anxious person is soothed in the presence of one more stable. A planner loves the spontaneity brought to their life from their partner, and the more laid-back person likes the way their partner pays their bills on time and keeps their credit score higher.

WHY CAN'T YOU BE MORE LIKE ME?

During times of stress, rather than appreciating the difference in "the other," there is an unspoken demand to do things "our" way.

Certainly, most couples hold many things in common, yet it is in negotiating the **differences** that we often find a relationship succeed or fail, particularly in the first years of a relationship.[13] In the tension of our differences, we can get into a competition over what is best according to our own standards and fight around "what is the right way."

Complementary relationships work well during times of low stress, but often become problematic when life hits challenges—which life often does.

One factor every couple must manage is that each partner has a distinct body. Each of these bodies move or don't move very well. Each body needs particular amounts of food, sleep, sex and attention to other physical processes or they don't function very well. Yet, most couples fail to recognize the day-to-day power of the physical aspects of their partnering, our sexual relationship being just one of many. Some of the newest brain imaging technology supports the finding that even parts of the brain (AKA: a body part) work a bit differently person to person.[14]

Many premarital preparation programs appear to overlook the fact that we take our bodies into our relationship. As a therapist who has worked with many couples, particularly around issues of health, the body can become a central player in a marriage or intimate relationship.

You may recall the example in the section on Myths about the differing food needs that my husband and I bring into our relationship. My hypoglycemic-body needs to have fuel intakes regularly or it does not function well (I can get light-headed and cranky), while my husband can go for hours without eating and cruise through the time in a steady manor.

Each of our bodies requires an owner's manual for good maintenance. Would you use a BMW owner's manual as a reference for fixing a Ford? Of course not! Yet we sometimes treat our partner as if they come from the exact same manufacturer. (OK you and your partner can now argue on who is the BMW and who is the Ford).

The Best Way to Start a Relationship: Know Thyself

The best situation would be for each partner to come into an intimate relationship very well versed in self-knowledge and body awareness. They would also be ready to learn about and care for what their partner brings. Each person would, in a sense, "know thyself" well and respect this in their partner too.

Here's a brief inventory to see how aware you are about yourself:
- How much sleep do you need to be alert and productive for the next day?
- What time of day do you think most creatively and work most productively?
- How much exercise or activity do you need in order to be functional and strong?
- How often do you need to eat? What types of food make you feel fatigued or energized? How much is too much alcohol or caffeine?
- How much touch, sensual activity and sexual contact do you need to feel alive?

- Do you struggle with ADHD, learning disabilities, depression or other mental health issues? How well are these managed in your life?
- When you have free time, how do you like to use it?
- What do you do when you're on the verge of a cold to bolster your immune system?
- What physical vulnerabilities do you have from your genetic and health histories (for example, diabetes, alcoholism, high blood pressure or cancer) that might come into play in your own life?

Ideally, in a solid partnership, each person comes into the relationship having a fairly good sense of these areas on their own. They have "become an adult" in these areas and no longer just do what they were taught growing up. A mature person learns new ways to behave through personal trial and error, input from good friends, or education. It is best to understand and practice behaviors that truly "fit" the body that you have.

Making Room for Each Body in Your Relationship

When couples do well with this area of life, each person must respect and make room for both people's biology. Our bodies require a certain amount of care, and without this care, we cannot function well. For a couple, this means that they cannot do everything the same way they did when they were single. There are several essential differences that couples must manage together. Some of these will have to do with how we sleep or what we choose to eat. Other differences will be more complex to manage, such as how our brains work differently; we do not absorb information from the world or make decisions in the exact same way. Since we need different things and process information differently, we may misunderstand what our partner needs or what we need from our partner. This can be interpreted as a lack of care. The bottom line is that each ME is unique; each partner must be respected and many aspects of their biology accepted if a relationship is to survive.

In the next few sections, I will highlight information to help you recognize some of the biological aspects behind Fight #1. I am not trying to do a complete review, but I want to give you some information to see how legitimate and easy it is to get caught up in this type of fight. I will then move to the particular skills (A-Skills) best suited to address Fight #1.

Ships passing in the night: Body clocks and biorhythms or...why are you going to bed when I'm waking up?

Over the past several decades, researchers and popular books have helped us to understand better how a person can match their biology to the activities they do.[15] A few studies even explore this within a couple's relationship.[16] For example, the divorce rate is actually higher for those who have opposite circadian rhythms than those who share circadian rhythms. So what's a circadian rhythm? OK, in basic terms: if you're a night owl and so is your partner, you'll have a better chance of making the relationship work than if one prefers to stay up late and one prefers to get up very early.[17]

Wake and sleep patterns as well as hormones released during the day shift how we function. A basic example: ever have a meeting right after a big lunch? Hard to stay awake, huh? In this case it is the fact that your body redirects your blood flow from your brain to your digestion, so you become less mentally alert. Melatonin is one brain chemical that has a lot to do with feeling sleepy. Some people have more and some have less in their bodies, thus the differences in sleep patterns. As people age, they can change in the amount of melatonin they produce, so this biological difference can become even more pronounced.[18]

The larger the gap a couple needs to manage between being "day" or "night" people, the more conflict they may have.

Here's an example:

> Rick and Carol were in a relationship for two years before they both decided to get married. While they shared excitement about the upcoming nuptials, they were both a little skeptical because there were times where they would argue. In their words, "We weren't on the same page." Through couples counseling, they determined that part of the reason they were having difficulties was because they couldn't get into a steady, conjoining rhythm of life, often having different work schedules and sleeping patterns. As a result, when Rick was tired, Carol was often very active while when Carol was exhausted, Rick was upbeat and ready to do something. Both had high expectations of doing things together and these conflicting biorhythms created stress in their relationship they could not explain. However, after hearing that these inconsistencies were normal and part of their biological differences, and that they could do small things to alter their schedules to become more congruent, they achieved a more in-sync relationship and eventually the marriage patterns fit better for both of them.

Research shows that when a couple's wake and sleep patterns do not align (night versus morning people), they experience less marital adjustment, more marital conflict, less time in shared conversation, less time shared in activities and less sexual activity than those couples who do match up. So your biological clock can really make a difference in how you have opportunities to partner with each other.[19]

Biorhythm may also be related to sexual interest. There are hormones related to sexual interest that fluctuate throughout the day. It appears that there is a specific section in our DNA that relates to our internal biorhythm clock. (OK for you biology nerds, this goes something like: the gene section impacts a protein synthesis that impacts the hypothalamus that activates the pituitary glands responsible to "turn on" our sex hormones). Some days the switch is fully on and some days you're more turned off.[20]

Since hormones impact our sexual drive (libido) and fluctuate throughout the day, partners can vary in their sexual interest. Matching levels of heightened libido can create more opportunities for mutually desired sexual encounters. When couples identified when they had sex with each other and, in addition, listed when they would have had sex "ideally" on their own time schedule, those couples who matched more closely in their real-ideal match also reported higher sexual satisfaction in their sexual relationship. Not rocket science.

But here's an interesting finding in the same study: when couples were asked to share their ideals to each other first and then begin to "work toward the other," they increased in their sexual satisfaction even if the "frequency count" did not change.[20]

So this leads us back to our Myth-Buster Chapter and the ME, the YOU, and the WE discussion. When couples are able to identify the ME (in this case, my ideal sexual frequency) and then to learn about the YOU (my partner's idea sexual frequency) and then together they place this information into a WE context (working towards our ideal sexual frequency together), the couple was more satisfied, *even when* the differences were not resolved.

Remember: addressing an issue does not require finding a solution. Particularly with fights connected to our biology, it is often **not about compromise**. Each person will not "give in" or "shift" who they are. Addressing Fight #1 is mostly about making emotional and physical "room" for each other's different biological needs. I will explain this more in the skill section related to Fight #1.

He said, She said: Hormones and the Brain

Yes hormones belong in this section on biology and couple fights. I remember seeing a woman's T-shirt that read, "Get out of my way. I'm out of estrogen and I've got a gun." I appreciated the warning, and so would her partner.

Remember, our particular biology provides us with a sort of working blueprint for who we are and who we become. Of course, biology is not the whole story. Other factors strongly shape us too, but for now let's review some findings about bodies and hormones.

One-year-old baby boys and girls were tested for the level of testosterone in their blood—yes, girls have testosterone too. And guess what? The lower the testosterone, the longer the baby would look at a human face and the higher the testosterone, the shorter the attention to the human face. The researchers summarized that most girl babies have "superior" socializing abilities right from the start and boys are at a disadvantage.[21] OK, so maybe that's because one-year-old babies have had some significant gender expectation input by that juncture, so maybe this is about nurture and not nature.

How about another example from biology? Newborn boy and girl babies in the hospital were given a face to look at and THEN given a mechanical mobile to look at. And, yes, you guessed it: most girls looked longer at the face and the boys looked significantly longer at the mobile![22]

Another convincing piece of evidence for the role of hormones in gender differences lies in a condition called adrenal hyperplasia. Mothers with this condition have high levels of testosterone during pregnancy and are more likely to give birth to girls with better spatial abilities as well as more aggressive behavior

An uninvited Y chromosome!

towards others, much more similar to young boy behavior.[23] In our politically correct, sometimes gender sensitive culture, it does make you think.

Finally, menstrual cycles would fit in the biology of Fight #1 too. Although less researched at the couple relational level, hormone fluctuations during some women's monthly cycle can impact how they feel and behave in their intimate relationships. Although research in some other cultures may not identify this disorder, in North America, those women who suffer from Premenstrual Dysphoric Disorder (PMDS) can be challenged by difficult physical and emotional symptoms. These hormone-related difficulties impact both partners and not just the woman alone.[24]

Idea for those suffering with PMDS:

As a clinician, I have at times encouraged a couple to hang up a monthly calendar in a shared living space. The woman with PMDS will place happy face stickers on the days most likely for her to deal with premenstrual symptoms in order to remind her partner. Menstrual cycle apps can help with tracking this too.

The couple makes a pact ahead of time to minimize decision-making or stressful events during these days of the month. They also create specific self-care and couple-care rituals for these days. For those couples that work at becoming a working unit to deal with this biological issue, tensions between them often diminish.

Are you my type? The hardwiring of temperament and a couple's relationship

Now we move to another important biological factor in relationships: personality. These differences are seen from birth and they just don't go away. Discussing personality helps us to distinguish how people operate differently in the world, probably due to their particular genetic make-up. The body comes to the fore again.

Temperament is a specific "piece" or aspect of personality that many researchers study. To use a computer analogy, are you more like a MAC or a PC? For example, brain-imaging technology finds that two people's brains might "light up" differently, even if they are shown the same item.[25]

Even though you and your partner may share and enjoy many similar things and function well together, there will be times that you won't. For example, what brings you relief when there is tension might be to talk about it; in contrast, talking could increase your partner's stress. Your partner might want to watch a TV show and not have a conversation as a way to relieve stress, while watching TV might heighten your frustration.

Let me offer a temperament example that I see often in my clinical practice...fights around socializing:

You had a hard day at work and come home wanting to get some space and watch your favorite show. You sit down and begin watching, then your partner comes home. He just got off the phone with his sister who is having medical tests—again. Your partner sits down to talk about the medical situation. You are interested but you also don't think it's an emergency. You know your partner needs to talk through things when he is upset. So, besides the stresses each of you has brought to the situation, you're both now feeling additional stress from your differences.

Does a party deplete you or energize you?

In the situation above, if one partner demands to reduce stress only in their way, the stress will get even worse. In fact, a cycle of interaction between the couple may then shift from the initial stresses to an argument of the differences in how each person copes. It might even move into evaluating "what stress" is more important. This competition does not help either partner or the relationship.

Understanding how you cope, that is, what you need to function in life when stress appears, is one aspect of your personality. Getting some sense of the pieces of your personality, or temperament, can help you become more self-aware and can help you and your partner make enough room to become a WE more effectively. The goal is to learn how to respond to and not react. The goal is also to make room for each person to get what they need.

RESEARCH SHOWS:

Videotaped longitudinal research studies from the Yale Child Development Laboratories describe how some aspects of personality are probably structured from birth.[26] The researchers studied very young babies and then followed them into childhood. Certain reactions of the infants predict how "social" the child would be several years later.

Here's what they did. The researchers placed a very intricate toy mobile over the infant who was sitting reclined in an infant seat. The babies were not even old enough to sit up on their own yet. The mobile had lots of stuff hanging down—mirrors and an assortment of colored toys. Two distinct reactions resulted from the mobile encounter: some babies would smile, relax their arms and look with interest at all the sensory input. Others, in contrast, would tense up, start to cry, try to turn away and bat at the toys so they would leave. These same babies were followed into preschool childcare settings and researchers could often accurately predict which toddlers loved to play with others, interact and talk with lots of people and which toddlers would strongly prefer to play alone and not verbalize or interact much. Any guess on which group matched which personality trait?

The infants who "enjoyed" all the input from the toy mobile showed extroverted behavior later in preschool while infants who were "overwhelmed" by the toy mobile showed introverted temperament characteristics. Extroverted preschoolers played with others more often, verbalized more readily and sought out making friends. Introverted children enjoyed spending time alone, happily playing by themselves and seemed fine with just one "best friend."

One common personality trait difference relates to the amount of social interaction that people need. Some people need a lot, and some very little. Certain people are quite content to spend hours by themselves, while others would get depressed if they were alone. We term the first introverts and the second extroverts. Most people are some mix of both.

To use a metaphor for this biology-driven personality characteristic, I think of an uncharged battery. Extroverts need people connection and verbal interchange to be re-charged, while introverts need time alone (or maybe with just one familiar friend) to re-charge. When people are out of balance in this domain, they will not function well.

So how is personality important in a couple's relationship?

At least for those married, one major contributor to a couple ending their relationship (next to a couple's unrealistic expectations) is their personality traits.[27] Some might interpret this to mean that certain people show traits that are undesirable, such as being impulsive. However, many personality traits are biological differences that a couple must manage in order to stay in the relationship.

Besides socializing preferences, people may manage their emotions differently as a result of their personality traits. If you've ever observed a nursery filled with babies, you will notice differences in emotional regulation. Some children seem to be content and happy, others irritable, others change from moment to moment. Each child seems to bring into the world a tendency in its emotional make-up. In a sense each individual has a thermostat or set-point in their inner workings, and each will have tendencies to warm up or cool down depending on their settings.

Of course life experiences can also impact strongly how emotions are regulated, but some emotional differences are strongly shaped by genetics.[28] For example, dopamine, a key brain chemical found in one's genetic code, is clearly associated with levels of anxiety in a person's desire to experience new things. Those who have certain types of brain chemicals exhibit more or less anxiety and these tie to how a person wants to explore or "not explore" the world around them.[29]

Serotonin, another key brain chemical is also involved in the emotional display of anxiety and depression. Although certainly not the entire story, the biology of anxiety and depression, the ability to self-soothe and manage new situations appears to be tied to person's biological tendencies from a very early age.[30] Of course, people are impacted by their life experiences and can also learn skills to cope with anxiety and depression. So let's turn to one final biological example.

Brain processing differences

Do you dream in color? Do you remember the phone number from the first house you lived in? Can you transport yourself to the memory of when you first kissed someone? Do class lectures bore you? Do you need activity to keep you engaged?

Detectives interviewing witnesses at a hit and run accident certainly report that people will notice the experience differently—some might notice the color of the car while another has no clue of the color but could repeat the sound of the loud thud when the person was hit.[31] It appears that brains vary in how they take in information from the world around them.[32]

This is true for couples too. Partners might experience the same event and take away very different pieces of information. A personal example for my husband and me is our weekly review of events. We usually chat and look at our calendars on Monday mornings to coordinate our upcoming week. If my husband doesn't write what we talked about down on his calendar (he tends to be a visual processor), then he can easily lose details from our verbal discussion. In contrast, I can often remember a conversation word by word. During a tense exchange, my husband will focus on the look on my face and I will notice the tone of his voice.

Some people may have more biological connections in the visual parts of the brain while others may be have more auditory processing capabilities. The impact is that each partner may differ in what they notice and this can lead to arguments and differences in how they communicate and make decisions.

Biology or Culture?

Many of you might ask at this juncture: so is the fight we are having more about biology (nature) or upbringing (nurture)? Is Fight #1 stemming from mainly biological or learned difference?

Evolutionary biologists argue that some differences have been shaped for thousands of years and have helped the human race to survive.[33] Of course theologians might argue that some differences might stem from being "created male and female."[34] Parents just might notice how little boys pick up sticks and make them into guns, while little girls pick up stray dogs and bring them home. Biology, behavior and culture association are intricately interconnected.

At this time, we don't yet know how to distinguish what is only biological and what is learned in persons, that is, what may be more "given" and what may be more "learned and changeable" in a person. A combination of both seems to make sense for most people. But what seems clear from much of this research related to Fight #1 is that the ***biology strongly influences*** how a person functions in their relationships. People can learn new things, but they may default into their biological comfort levels when stress increases.

The bottom line for Fight #1 is that biology does play an influential role in how each partner functions and some of the biological differences will show up in the tensions we have with each other. These biological differences are often legitimate needs and often not very changeable. A couple must make room for each person in order for each to function well within the relationship. So now let's turn to the skills needed for Fight #1.

Fight #1

A's

Fight #1
A-Skills

- **Awareness with Acceptance**
- **Add-to: Use Ands to Expand**
- **Appreciation through Affirmation**

Fight Skill: Awareness and acceptance of differing needs

You must acknowledge that individual differences exist and become aware that the YOU *is not* the ME. Do not pretend that you and your partner are the same—you aren't. Acceptance, at its root, is the ability to respect that some characteristics in your partner will *not* change and are not the way you do, experience, need or see things. In fact, some of these differences are evidence of your uniqueness.

Acceptance means that you have come to terms with the fact that, in some areas of life, it is OK that your partner won't change.[35]

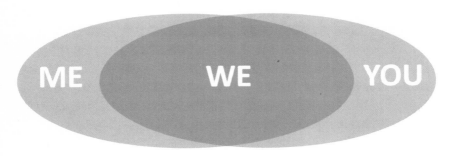

THE WE IS VITAL

Fight Skill: Add to (Don't compromise— EXPAND)

This fight skill is about broadening the possibilities and not averaging them out. It is not about an economic model of win-win. The opportunity is a creative exercise to find a way that you both can live within and to care about the basic differences that you bring to the relationship. Try to expand the WE. Use the word "AND" a lot.

DO make room for both: take one car together at the beginning of the party AND then call an UBER for the one who wants to leave earlier since you socialize differently.

DON'T average sleep time and keep the expectation that you need to go to bed and sleep together at all times. Neither of you would feel rested.

DO expand the way your prepare meals so that each person is able to eat the things that help them function well.

DON'T expect each person to enjoy the same things.

DO watch TV without talking AND take time to talk as well.

Fight Skill: Appreciate and affirm since the complement can synergize

A good response for addressing Fight #1 is to respond to differences by saying "that's him" or "that's her" rather than "you're wrong" or "you're bad." Appreciate individuality since you may find that the characteristic that is a hassle now may be helpful later in life. Differences often enrich a relationship in the long run, although they can truly bother you along the way. Life will change and different skills will fit better at different stages. For example, more flexible personalities may be very useful when your children become teens, but a more structured personality may work best in parenting elementary aged children.

Learn to compliment your partner for the way your partner "complements" your relationship. That is, let your partner know how their differences help you at times. For example, if you struggle with paying bills on time, thank your partner for being careful about your money. For those who have a difficulty being spontaneous, thank your partner when they bring some surprise and unexpected fun into your life.

Remember the WE perspective talked about in Myth-Buster chapter? Together in their differences, a couple can be stronger and will be able to manage a range of life difficulties better than a person will do just on their own. At a particular point in time, one partner's way of doing things might be more effective, but over a lifetime of demands, the resources of more than one person's style will help a couple and family cope the best.

EXERCISES FOR FIGHT #1

1. List some "biological fights" that you have with your partner.
   - Biorhythms
   - Temperament traits (introvert/extrovert)
   - Remembering details of an experience differently

2. Use an on-line personality inventory and compare notes with your partner.

3. Circle any of the fights you and your partner have had that are on this list.
   - Food preferences
   - How long to take a shower
   - Amount of touch
   - How many naps
   - How much exercise to get
   - How much you drink alcohol
   - If your clothes are smelly or not

4. Identify and try to map the interaction you and your partner have had using an example of Fight #1. List the topic. Who says what? How does each person react? Now try to give a compliment to your partner about some of these differences.

5. Can you give an example of a way you and your partner have "added to both" so that you can get more of what you need?

6. For a week, try to compliment your partner when they do or say something "unique" to them. Notice your interactions change. Notice how you change toward your partner.

"I'm not so sure I'll feel comfortable
hanging out with your family."

FIGHT #2

"Why can't you be more like my family?"
or Different Generational Legacies

All couple relationships are cross-cultural—but, you need to figure out just how cross-culturally different you are.

I remember the first "big fight" my husband and I had. It was about dirty socks. Yes, dirty socks. It had to do with where dirty socks are supposed to live when they are dirty. My idea was that dirty socks were supposed to live in the laundry hamper in the bathroom immediately after they were taken off. My husband thought that dirty socks should live next to the bed at night while he was sleeping.

So take an inventory for a moment:
- Do you wash dishes from the right to left or left to right and how clean is clean anyway?
- Does the toilet paper drape over the roll or under the roll? (Over the roll, duh!)

- Is a work bonus check seen as "fun money" or to be "stashed away for a rainy day?"
- Are children to be indulged or disciplined?
- Are you supposed to buy your relative the "perfect gift" or stay within a budget?
- And how many days can you stay with your in-laws without going crazy, really?

Size does matter. Are we negotiating a little or a lot?

I regularly joke with my students that graduate school is really "expensive vocabulary." What I mean by this is that each professional discipline trains their new recruits in a particular language. The words of our academic disciplines help us to make sense of the world. For example, if I were to offer reasons for higher crime rates in a community, I might talk about the stresses on family structure, but a sociologist might talk about racism and marginalization, or an economist might note increased economic globalization or a theologian might talk about social justice.

Expensive vocabulary in this section brings us to the words *heterogamy* and *homogamy*. Often related to divorce rates, these terms look at how size does matter. *The more differences between the families that the individuals come from, the more challenges the couple will have.*[36] Generally couples divorce or break-up less when they come from more similar backgrounds. This includes levels of education, economic status, religion and ethnic background. A couple must negotiate more or less depending on their differences. Thus, some couples are challenged more from the very start of their relationship to be able to work out the WE of their relationship.

Love me, love my family: Culture clashes at every turn

Fights around daily living often stem from the family and cultural messages and behaviors that we have absorbed since childhood. We tend to judge another when they don't do it our way. We seem to constantly "judge" how well our partner does things our familiar, that is, our family, way. Remember my dirty socks example?

A core reason why we "fight poorly" is that when others think or act differently than us, we don't know how to stay connected within these differences. We criticize the other who is different and don't attend to what we are bringing into the situation. Often individuals can't seem to maintain a sense of self while staying close to another who is different. Therapists call these boundary issues[37] where we need to figure out and become comfortable with where one individual ends and the other one begins.

When we get mad, we usually distance ourselves or criticize the other person. In both cases, there is a movement away. When we are angry, we put up a barrier between ourselves and the other person. We react in particular ways—often "flight" or "fight." When someone is mad, we naturally move away physically or emotionally to *protect ourselves*. This dynamic is very common but often misunderstood.

The more differences between the families that the individuals come from, the more challenges the couple will have.

AN EXAMPLE OF DIFFERENT CULTURES

Ahmed and Christie met in college. They lived in the same dorm complex for two years, shared many classes and loved to go out to the movies and coffee shops together. They fell in love and began to live together in their senior year. Talk about marriage became serious. It was at that time that Ahmed's family moved to the same city. His close-knit family expected Ahmed to spend at least one day every weekend with them and to attend all birthday and special holiday celebrations. Although Christie was invited too, there were times that she was not. The opportunities for movies and coffee shops decreased. Christie asked Ahmed to not feel obligated to be with his family as often, but he felt torn between his love of family and love of her. They reported feeling more distant from each other and angry outbursts, new to their relationship, began to occur on a regular basis. Some of Christie's friends suggested that she ask Ahmed to choose between her and his family. Instead, she came into therapy and, after the first visit, the therapist asked her to consider bringing Ahmed in too. He agreed to come in, and in the next session, they began to explore the powerful family patterns each were bringing into the relationship that they had not considered before.

Anger is an energizing emotion—it calls for action. As a couple's therapist, I see signs of anger as very useful information—it helps me understand how each person is different and that the couple has not negotiated those differences very well. They have not learned the elements of "wise prize-fighting" discussed in the earlier Myth-buster Chapter. Each person is fighting for their individual way of doing things and has not learned to become a team player yet.

If anger is not acknowledged, it can go underground and show up in physical symptoms such as raised blood pressure, depression or skin related stress disorders like hives or psoriasis.[38] These days, most people understand that stress will impact their physical health. Anger can also become explosive and erupt into domestic violence.[39]

Anger can be a protective movement away from another who is different

In this section, we review ways that a fight stems from the differences in family legacies or generational patterns. In order to manage these fights more effectively, a couple needs to negotiate a NEW boundary that incorporates the best of BOTH partner's backgrounds.

THIS is how you SHOULD do it: Household habits

For about a decade I had a favorite wedding gift that I bought for my friends who were getting married: a ceramic toothpaste squeezer. Yes, tacky I know, but I included a note in the nice wedding wrap to say that I was saving them from one daily couple fight: the HOW to squeeze the toothpaste out of the toothpaste tube fight. You know this one: "You SHOULDN'T squeeze the tube in the middle but roll it up from the bottom" versus the "who cares as long as the toothpaste gets on my toothbrush?" battle.

Or maybe yours is the toilet seat up or down fight.

Or where to put the kitchen sponge after you're done washing the dishes?

As we partner with another, many small and large tensions can be recounted about becoming a WE in the relationship: from when to pay bills, where to spend holidays, how to clean the home, who to invite over for a meal or how to parent our children. There are countless differences in patterns learned through our differing families and our differing cultures, and often passed down over several generations.

As we begin to partner, we notice these differences frequently: like how "on-time" a person arrives at an event or how a person eats their food. However, after the "best behavior beginning" of a relationship, most people begin to show up more authentically and honestly. The tensions usually mildly increase in the relationship and if there are too many, the early-budding relationship often ends. However, when the relationship continues, it becomes easier to see differences between the families and patterns of each partner. Some of the differences will get incorporated into your new couple relationship and some will not.

So think about your relationship for a moment and list two or three places where your differences have been noticed? (A few are listed in the exercises at the end of this chapter).

She does the laundry; he mows the lawn? Gender role expectations in coupling

Messages about gender are central in these family and cultural differences. What are the messages that you receive because you are "male" or "female" (some cultures even make room for more than these two genders)?[40] Reflect a moment on the messages you received growing up about being a girl or a boy.

Research informs us that gender plays a very prominent part in relationship satisfaction and conflict. For example, husbands with traditional gender role attitudes experience more conflict with wives about relationship issues and decision-making than more egalitarian husbands. Also, traditional gender roles are found to have been linked to less ability for men to express emotion, which can lead to depression or decreased well being, and can be related to lower marital satisfaction.[41] Fathers who share more evenly in parenting and household tasks with their spouses report more satisfying marriages, better sex and closer relationships with their children throughout their lives.[42]

And when children are involved, how is each person expected to negotiate the responsibilities or work life and family life? If a partner comes from a more rigid versus flexible model, the couple must negotiate more tensions and disappointment.

An example:

> Tommy and Amanda had done well when first married,
> both supporting the other's career. However, when
> their first child was born, they were having all sorts of
> problems. Growing up in a family where his father was
> the breadwinner and his mother was a stay at home wife,
> Tommy was used to this type of family structure and
> believed this model was how his newly expanded family
> would automatically structure itself. Amanda, in contrast,
> grew up in a household where both her mother and father
> worked outside the home and shared household duties.
> Because of their different upbringings, the two of them
> were reluctant to accommodate each other and this led to
> marital arguments and much dissatisfaction.

In times of economic upheaval, paying attention to gender
expectations is particularly important since families often need
two incomes to thrive and/or one breadwinner can lose their job.
In increasing cases, the woman is contributing the larger amount
of income and benefits toward the family. Having more flexibility
to negotiate how to survive is quite useful for many couples.
Literature on the benefits and complexities of stay at home dads is
increasing with each year.[43]

You call it love, I call it suffocating: Closeness and distance in families & friendships

I was doing premarital counseling with a couple. She was younger and came from a very tight-knit family; he was divorced and spent more time outside his immediate family when he was growing up. This couple often got into a fight around spending time with her family. He called it "suffocating."

I had each of them draw a line on their own piece of paper. On one side I had them write, Do Things Together and the other side, Do Things Apart.

DO THINGS TOGETHER   **DO THINGS APART**

Without showing their partner, I asked them to put a mark on the place on the line that represented the way they grew up with the label (FOO=Family of Origin). Then I asked them to put a mark on the line where they wanted their relationship to be (with the label FOC=Family of Choice). She put her FOO mark on the extreme left side and put the FOC toward the middle. He put his FOO mark on the extreme right side and put the FOC toward the middle. Their marks ended up very close to each other.

I told them that they were negotiating "interdependence" which is the goal of a good marriage. They needed to figure out their own hopes for how to be both separate and connected. They smiled; both remarked how they appreciated how each brought a difference into their own couple relationship. Although they experienced tension in their differences at times, they were grateful for the closeness-distance reminders that each contributed. In particular, the exercise helped them see and experience that they BOTH contributed to the situation and that it wasn't only "her suffocating extended family" that was at play in their fight.

A core task for each couple is to negotiate closeness and distance in their relationship.[44] This negotiation applies not only to family connections but also to friendships, to work and to other outside activities. As people partner, they must re-negotiate many connections that they developed as a single person and move toward sharing their time and energies with their partner AND these other relationships. Differences in the balance of closeness and distance come into the center of many early tensions and arguments between couples. This closeness-distance dance reemerges throughout life, particularly in times of transition.

The Simpsons meet the Kardashians: When family values collide

Values show up in all areas of life, but usually in subtle ways. For example, when a teenager gets a driver's license, one parent might emphasize the need to get a job to pay for the added cost of insurance, while another might encourage more engagement in volunteer activities since these would look good on a college application. Families vary in their prizing of money versus education.

When the same adolescent gets money from a job or from a gift, values might be seen in an expected contribution to the larger family income or in the brand of clothes purchased. Depending on their socioeconomic status, couples can bring subtle or obvious differences into their life negotiations.

While money tension can be due to any of the three fights noted in the book, the most common one stems from family values around financial behaviors and decisions. A phrase such as "You can't take it with you" falls on deaf ears when said to a "Save it for a rainy day" type person. How each person talks about money, spends money and saves/invests money are windows into the values each holds. Example 2 in the first chapter of this book gives one example of this. When a couple become parents, values around the child's needs versus the larger family needs come into focus; it is not uncommon for one parent to be more child-centered and the other to be less so.

Couples will need to negotiate an array of values including social (e.g., what it looks like to be respectful), political (e.g., conservative vs. progressive), moral (e.g., telling the truth), work (e.g., income production vs. time-off), and spiritual/religious (e.g., answering the question, what is life for anyway?). Some couples even choose to write their own Couple or Family Mission Statement, similar to organizations, in order to clarify what is most meaningful for them.[45]

The way each person talks about money, spends money and saves/invests money reveals each of their values.

Now We're Getting Serious: Family Rituals

Another major area of tension comes when couples negotiate rituals, that is, shared activities that hold special meaning. Much of what people hold as important, even sacred—eating turkey at Thanksgiving, watching the Super Bowl together with family and friends, attending religious services, giving particular types of gifts, eating specific foods at holidays, including a Chuppah at a wedding ceremony, celebrating birthdays—are associated with a rich host of feelings, memories, meanings, behaviors and history. As humans, we're deeply connected to questions of life's purpose. These areas are strongly tied to culture.

Couples are often challenged to pick and choose what rituals to keep in and what to leave out. Couples who come from different religious traditions can find this to be particularly challenging.[46]

For example:

> It was four months before the wedding. Everyone was on edge. The economic and religious differences between Tracy and Todd began to show up at every turn. Tracy grew up in an affluent, Catholic home; Todd was raised culturally Jewish by a single parent that struggled to pay the bills. Both longed to create a very special day to mark their commitment of marriage, and had found a perfect venue in the large backyard of a close friend. However, the costs associated with each food choice for the reception became a huge source of disagreement and the music each suggested for the ceremony was met by silence or reactivity. Both had shared with close friends that they sometimes wondered if they should call the wedding off.

It is not unusual for rituals like wedding ceremonies or religious holidays to be a source of significant tension for many couples. These differences often spill out into extended family relationships as well. It is in the tension of the couple's different upbringing that you might hear the phrase, *Why Can't You Be More Like My Family?*

So now let's turn to the fight skills needed for Fight #2.

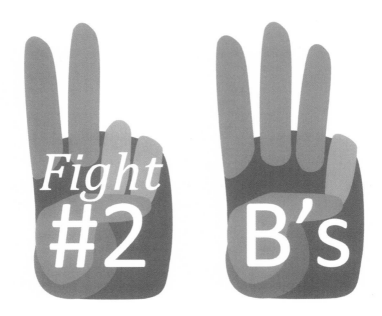

Fight #2 B's

Fight #2
B-Skills

- **Be Patient**
- **Become an Intentional Negotiator**
- **Balance the WE, YOU & ME**

Fight Skill: Be Patient

Begin by holding realistic expectations for the amount of couple conflict you will likely experience. Answer the question honestly: how different are our family backgrounds, a little, a moderate amount, or quite a lot? If you don't know, then you need to become an explorer. You'll need to ask questions of your partner and your partner's family members and friends. Become a detective and pay attention to patterns and unspoken messages that often lie underneath reactions to tense discussions with your partner or your partner's family.

I love Google Earth. I love watching as the pictures move from an individual home, to street level to neighborhood, to community, to city, to state, to region, to country, to a global perspective. The process of stepping back to get the broader view is central for a couple's relationship to succeed and survive. You need know where you are starting from. Take time to explore the many layers of connection in your relationship and the larger world in which you live and were raised.

Fight Skill: Become an Intentional Negotiator

Ideally, each partner will participate in a conscious development of the new WE. Otherwise, a partnership can get stuck in a reactive struggle of fighting for one's own way, or their family's way.

This fight skill is associated with loyalty and honest negotiation—you have now committed yourself to your partner and not just to your family of origin. You may need to let go and wake up to the fact that it is not just about you or the family you grew up in, it's about your couple relationship NOW. What are you really fighting for, the past, the present or the future? Foundationally, whose side are you on? Now re-read Myth Buster 3 on page 31.

The goal for you as a couple is to create a NEW system perspective, that is, a blend of the best of both your histories in order to make a more satisfying relationship in the present and build a shared future. You've got to take your plane off auto-pilot (the programming from your family history) and take over the wheel so you are consciously choosing where you want to fly. Your NEW combination system can be better than your combined pasts. Talk about your hopes. Discuss your expectations. express what you value, listen well, and attempt to be flexible. You will be able negotiate a shared experience when you have enough information from your partner ahead of time. In the moment, usually reactivity rules, so spend a bit of time before major events to discuss your wishes and preferences.

Fight Skill: Balance the WE, YOU & ME.

The individual, family and couple concerns are all battling for priority as we partner. There is no perfectly right decision and there is rarely a simple one. Healthy commitment in an intimate relationship moves from a sense of "only ME" to a commitment to a "WE." This means you have to be willing to not get your way and to work on what will work for BOTH of you. This may mean that you compromise, give in, play quid pro quo, take turns, and even stand your ground occasionally while at the same time responding with care to your partner's frustrations and concerns.

For couples to survive, they have to take a bigger picture perspective. This is a non-narcissistic and non-selfish way to live, and it requires deep honesty from each person. You need to say what you mean and what you feel, you need to describe these thoughts and feelings to the other and risk being challenged by them. Most couples do not do this very well; the first surge of divorce occurs during the first few years of the relationship when the core of the WE is being developed.

REMEMBER: Moving from a ME to a WE takes time

EXERCISES FOR FIGHT #2

1. Identify one or two things that you cherish most about the family you grew up in. Identify one or two things that you did not like about the family you grew up in.

KEEP	DO DIFFERENTLY

Is the emotional connection stronger for your positive or negative memory? Share these ideas with your partner.

2. Describe a typical day in your life when you were about 8 years old and again when you were a teenager. Share these stories with your partner. What patterns do you see from these "past timeframes" that continue in your life right now?

3. Identify two examples of Fight #2 from your relationship.

4. How were boys and girls treated in your family? Were there any differences? What expectations were there for a male or female in your family growing up? If there were not gender differences, what about sibling position? Did older children have different responsibilities that younger ones? Did expectations change over time?

5. Continuum of connection: (graph yourself on this line at age 8 and 16).

DO THINGS TOGETHER   **DO THINGS APART**

6. Continuum of family rules (graph your family on this line at 8 and 16).

FEW RULES   **MANY RULES**

7. Discuss some ways you would like to continue patterns and traditions from your upbringing into your future.

8. Discuss some ways that you would like to do things differently from your upbringing.

FIGHT #3

"Why can't you understand my hurt?"
or Different Relational Pain

Can't you see that you need to read the fine print?

Wait a minute, I didn't sign up for this. There was fine print?

"I am just so sad," Rose said in a trembling voice. She could barely look up during the therapy session. "I feel so small and unimportant." The voice of this 38-year old woman sounded like she was about 6 years old.

We all carry injuries from our past, some more damaging than others. We live in an unkind world and we all have been treated harshly or neglectfully at times. In the best of families, things are not perfect. Even if our family was fairly functional, we have other intimate relationships with friends or previous partners that bring pain into our lives.

Sue Johnson puts this well:

> From the cradle to the grave, humans desire a certain someone who will look out for them, notice and value them, soothe their wounds, reassure them in life's difficult places and hold them in the dark.[47]

We see evidence of this desire for a safe place in movies like Tyler Perry's 2005 *Diary of a Black Woman*. When Orlando proposes marriage, he says:

> "You've been through so much. I don't want to see you hurt anymore. Now I may not be able to give you all that you're used to. But I do know I can love you past your pain. I don't want you to worry about anything. You just wake up in the morning, that's all you have to do and I'll take it from there. There's one condition. You have to be my wife."[48]

Or in songs, like Justin Timberlake's "Not a Bad Thing" (2014)

> I know people make promises all the time
> Then they turn right around and break them
> When someone cuts your heart open with a knife and you're bleeding
> But I could be that guy to heal it over time
> And I won't stop until you believe it
> 'Cause baby you're worth it[49]

At a 50% divorce rate, something must be going terribly wrong. Didn't the book or movie say I was to live happily ever after? Even that magazine article said that married couples live, on the average, four years longer than single people. So what's up with these horrible feelings?

Most couples do not understand that fight #3 is central to the major "work" of being in an intimate relationship.

Most people do not enter into a marriage or committed relationship with a clear understanding of the pain aspect of the "couple contract." They haven't read the fine print.

As a result of reaching out and getting close to another person, you will often suffer what psychotherapy researchers term "secondary trauma." That is, when you emotionally connect to your partner, some of the pain of their experiences will spill out and onto you. You will be negatively impacted from some of the difficult history that your partner brings to you. Some of this pain will probably be raw and reactive and not even conscious. This is certainly not fair to you, but it is very real.

A personal example:

Early in our marriage, my husband would become irritated a few days before I would leave for an academic conference. He would ask me why I had to be away for so many days and if I really needed to go. He would "tease me" about his being neglected, and mention that he wouldn't eat very well while I was gone. There was humor in his tone, but also something else. Several years into our marriage, my husband told me a story. When he was about 5 years old, all his family had gone for a picnic at a park and they had played together during the afternoon. When they were ready to leave, his parents decided to play a little trick: to hide from him without letting him know. I still heard a tinge of hurt while he recounted the story. He still remembered the fear that surged in his body when he recognized that his family was nowhere to be seen. After a few moments alone, the family came out of hiding. They were laughing and thought it was a joke; they minimized his scared feelings as he reunited with them. But these feelings of abandonment stuck.

In a sense, Fight #3 is about the existential and spiritual aspects of coupling.[50] We all attempt to bring meaning to our lives. When we partner well with another in their pain, we help them to heal and at the same time we develop our own character. We can become more patient, more understanding, and more accepting.

I come from a worldview that says that life has purpose and carrying the suffering of another in this world is one aspect of a having a meaning-filled life.

However, we can respond reactively to our partner's pain or distance from it in order to protect ourselves. It is very difficult to tolerate this pain, particularly when it is directed at us. When we respond reactively, we bring the history of the pain into the present relationship and can compound the suffering for both parties.

Fight #3 has to do with the existential and spiritual aspects of coupling.

Fight #3 also ties to our biological wiring and our ability to mirror and experience empathy. When we "mirror" the emotion of another (like when you smile at a baby who smiles at you), we begin to be emotionally in-tune with them. Empathy allows a person's brain to experience the powerful effect of being validated in their skin. When we work to have compassion for another, we develop a shared intimacy.

It is important to note that, in some people, the biological capacity to mirror emotions might be damaged, such as in autism spectrum disorder.[51] But most people are born with the ability to mirror the emotion of another. Individuals can even choose to improve their ability to empathize. During training, most psychotherapists work on the skill of "empathic attunement." Like tuning the dials of a radio receiver, you can work to clear out the static in the radio waves and tune more clearly into the emotional signal being sent to you.

Empathy often begins the emotional connection to another, but compassion keeps us present in the midst of the suffering. Lori Chandler in her blog, *BigThink*, offers a wonderful way to distinguish empathy from compassion. Empathy is a gateway to compassion while compassion is empathy in action.[52] The ability to connect with empathy and compassion is central to the work of Fight #3 and brings life and healing to our relationships. More insight into the practices of empathy and compassion is found in the skill section related to this chapter.

Why this fight is particularly relevant now

Historically, the major job of family and couple life was survival— finding shelter, putting food on the table, birthing enough children for the next generation to do the same and to take care of older family members at the end of life. Modern society shifts the purpose of coupling from survival to emotional partnering. Unfortunately, many couples see relationships as an economic exchange versus a commitment *in sickness and in health* and *for better, for worse.*

There is a challenge in relationship definitions these days—similar to the Chinese symbol for change—which means both crisis ***and*** opportunity. We are less secure in our lives ***and*** yet we have more choices. We live in a society that is in the midst of many transitions—political threats, economic uncertainty, job changes, requirements to adjust to a new community after moving, unequal educational systems, and challenges to traditional religious beliefs. All of these lead to insecure attachments to the social systems and people around us.

In more developed countries, smaller-sized families are the norm. When there are fewer people to do the same number of tasks, this puts more demands on those who are present and can create higher expectations and stress on everyone.

Simultaneously, new social options are available for women as well as for men—many of which are becoming accepted and appreciated. There is a gift in the freedom of being able to choose, but there is increased uncertainty as well. Couples must navigate this new social frontier together, and this is easier said than done.

An example:

> Sarah and Troy married four years ago. Both have satisfying careers and they are trying to get pregnant. However, tense conversations have begun between them. Troy, raised by a single mother who lives several states away, feels loyal since she had sacrificed so much for him. He has asked Sarah to consider moving closer to his Mom when they begin having children since this would bring great joy to his Mom and she is willing to do childcare for free. Sarah, however, distrusts Troy's relationship with his Mom. She feels that Troy's mother is too needy. Sarah wants to prioritize their couple relationship. She had grown up with alcoholic parents who regularly forgot to pick her up from elementary school. She felt like she raised herself and his attention to his Mom seems almost like a betrayal. Troy reassures Sarah verbally, but still attends to his mother's wishes. He feels stuck between the two people he loves. Sarah often feels unloved by Troy's responses and unheard when she suggests that they stay in the city where they live now, where they may not have many social supports, but her job prospects are better. The tensions feel complex and unresolvable.

Let's unpack this example regarding Fight #3. Troy still carries strong emotional legacies from his family. He is experiencing deep sadness (that he really can't identify) since both his attachment relationships—to his wife and to his mother—are meaningful to him. He doesn't see a way to manage both. In contrast, Sarah comes from a family that neglected her at times and feels irritated and angry when Troy responds in a way that does not focus on her wishes and his attachment to her. At a deeper level, she feels anxious that Troy cannot love her the way she needs to be loved. Due to her background, she does not really consider herself loveable. If this couple came for couple's counseling, it would be very useful to explore each partner's history and attachment needs in order to work more productively on their marriage and their future plans.

The limits and benefits of pre-marital and relationship development programs

It is amazing to me that most states require some sort of written test and behind the wheel experience before people can legally drive and hold a license (that is, be responsible for driving a vehicle), but few states require any sort of relationship knowledge or experience before getting a marriage license. Yet, the damage from divorce is staggering; the social costs of divorce impact our health, family life and work productivity.[53]

I believe that pre-marital and/or pre-engagement counseling should be required for couples seeking a marriage license. Some states discount the fees for a marriage license when couples go through a premarital counseling experience (see *The National Healthy Marriage Resource Center* for a list of these states and the discounts available).[54] This is a step in the right direction.

Pre-marital counseling can be very helpful, allowing couples to identify strengths and challenges. When relationship expectations are more realistic, partnering goes better. Couples learn basic skills to address their issues proactively rather than reactively. Occasionally, people even postpone their wedding due to what they discover, which is probably helpful for everyone in the long run.

It is important that couples receive skills-based premarital counseling (not information-only programs).[55] The couple needs to actively participate in discussions and interactions together.

Many premarital and relationship counseling programs are limited because they rarely touch the deeper emotional longings and often-hidden emotional needs in the relationship. "Shared suffering" is not a content area in many of these programs! Content areas such as financial planning and personality compatibility are useful, but many relationships disintegrate due to under-addressed emotional and relational hopes and expectations within the relationship. Most of these difficult issues come from past pain, particularly unacknowledged family or relationship legacies.

Before addressing some examples of common and more subtle areas of relationship pain that partners bring into a relationship, let's start with the solution—*what is the best response to Fight #3?*

We must pause and just be with our partner in the pain.

The key: Intimacy built from empathy and compassion

Empathy and compassion are practices, not just ideas, they are the "how to" manuals for sharing pain and suffering. Empathy helps us tune into the emotions of another; and when we turn empathy into action we can truly care for another. We might notice small responses, like a glance at the floor or a deep sigh. We recognize that something more might be going on. We stop what we are doing. We may attempt to match what is going on in the other or we might get curious and ask gentle questions: "That was a big sigh," or "Are you OK?"

Compassion engages our own experience once we come alongside our partner. We feel with the other and imagine times when we have experienced something similar. We do not impose our experience on our partner, but we use the emotional understanding of that time to express our connection to them. Often, we just need to stand beside the person and take time to share in what they're feeling; in this way, we normalize the experience and it becomes a "me too" event. In fact, if we move quickly to "fix" the feeling, explain why it might be there or offer advice, our partner may feel alone in it, even if we are physically present. We must pause and just *be with* our partner in the pain.

Keep in mind that it takes time for most people to rely on each other at this deeper level. Particularly for those who have a more traumatic history, showing pain is difficult. People often work hard to "look good" on the outside, even when they feel vulnerable and anxious underneath. It makes sense for those who have been raised in mistrust to take time to develop trust.

AND it takes time to heal. The research from UCLA faculty member, Dr. Allan Schore, helps us see how the brain responds to the complexity of human interactions.[56] Dr. Schore suggests that it may take around 5 years of empathic and compassionate interactions for an anxiously attached person to become more secure in their life.

The good news is that the brain can "re-wire" (sometimes associated with the term, "brain plasticity") toward healthier functioning *through* the healing presence of another caring person.[57] Sometimes people heal through a significant relationship with a therapist, **but one of marriage's hidden secrets is that healthy partnering can bring healing too.**

As a couple develops more emotional responsiveness between them, their level of security and intimacy improves. The positive human interaction rewires the brain and moves the person who feels insecure to a place of security. As a person feels more secure, they will respond more productively within the relationship. A healthier collaboration can turn into the norm—or the other way around.

Of course, the bad news is that many couple relationships fail before they get to this point. *They didn't read the fine print.* So how does the pain related to Fight #3 develop?

Common Areas of "Traumatic Pain"

You knew this when you married me

> Most people do share some of their painful past when they begin to get to know their partner. However, these stories are often not well understood and their power is often underestimated. The triggers of this difficult history are often not rational and are not identified easily by the couple.

Hurt people hurt people

Abuse histories aren't just history. Patterns of verbal, physical or sexual abuse and neglect are deeply imbedded in people and are often not recognized. I have heard many stories from people who did not "perceive" the treatment they endured as abuse or neglect. They then acted in the same way with their children. Also, abuse can be experienced indirectly. We witness the violence between our parents even if it was not directed at us. These experiences can lead to unspoken fears within our current relationships.

OMG it might happen again

Loss from death, illness, divorce or financial setback can be traumatic. The loss of familiar connections, the inability to function physically, or the need to adapt to a lower standard of living impacts people at many levels. Any of these adjustments can cause grief or despair. Even though we often undervalue grief in American culture, we out not minimize this pain. Sometimes those who experience loss fear its reoccurrence so much that it limits their ability to enjoy life. At every turn, the anxiety of "it might happen again" resounds.

Don't make the same mistake twice or the "I will never" vows we make

Addictions aren't just an individual problem, they instill relational dynamics such as co-dependency are learned. When Janice was 9, she vowed to herself that she would never marry an alcoholic like her father. She married a man with a pornography addiction despite her efforts to avoid addicted people. Often tied to vows we make as young children—"I will never" or "I will always" commitments— can backfire as the emotional focus to protect ourselves sometimes makes us blind to other dimensions in the relationship.

How do I know you won't cheat?

When I was in 4th grade, my best friend of eight years found another best friend. I was hurt deeply and it took many years for me to be able to trust female relationships again. Fortunately, the gifts of several women friends have helped to heal this in me. The trauma of past infidelity and betrayal comes from friendships, work partners, and family relationships as well as from infidelity within the current relationship. We protect ourselves from getting too close so that we will not experience the pain again, but unfortunately, the cost of this response is that we miss out on intimacy, which requires a level of risk and letting others get close.

Common Areas of "Subtle Pain"

But they loved me

> Loving families that function well provide both structure and warmth, they meet the practical needs of shelter and food while also attending to the emotional and attachment needs of their members. However, some families do well in one domain and not very well in another. Many of the therapy students I train share stories of how their families "looked good" on the outside (they had a nice house, clothes, did well in school), but were lacking in emotional bonding and connections. Their parents practically parented, but did not attune emotionally very well. They were longing for this emotional connection they wanted and planned to focus on this for the clients they served.

The Perfect Family

> All families hold expectations, but some hold a standard for the expectation that is very controlling and even perfectionistic. We often see this in connection to eating disorders. Families pay attention to eating and weight gain in very precise and specific ways. They don't eat bread and they exercise everyday. They remark when clothes begin to be a little tight (even when it's due to a normal growth spurt) or when a stomach is relaxed. Much of this is communicated in non-verbal ways, such as judging looks or raised eyebrows. Those from perfectionistic families often become extra-sensitive to the nonverbal reactions of those around them.

But we need a doctor in the family!

If you were born into a family that managed a family business, say a restaurant, there would probably be pressure to help the family make the business work. You would be expected to "fill-in" on the weekends or holidays. This example is straightforward, but many families intentionally or unintentionally limit the exploration of life choices due to the larger family's standards or earlier family experiences. During college, one of my dormmates took his life; his suicide note to his Mom said that he was failing his course on anatomy. He believed that he would not get into medical school. The tragic note ended with: "I know you can never be proud of me." Messages about what is OK or not OK to explore significantly influence all of our development.

Only two can fit in this bed

You've probably heard the terms—Mama's boys or Daddy's girls. The connections between mothers and sons and fathers and daughters can be beautiful. However, at times, particularly in heterosexual couples, the expectations around being treated "special"—like a Prince or Princess— can interfere with the couple relationship. There is difficult work to be done in forming the couple unit particularly when unspoken family rules and anxiety impact your desire to do so. Loyalty to a family connection might compete with the loyalty to the partner. Who is in the bed anyway?

Boys don't do that

Gender messages are pervasive in our culture. From birth, boy babies are held in the arms of their parents differently than girl babies. Both subtle and overt expectations shape us, and we often don't even recognize them. In Fight #2, I talked about gender messages as influencing our actions. In Fight #3, the emphasis is on the underlying emotional needs of each partner. Many men in Western society are expected to "stay strong" and defend themselves. As a result, the human parts of us that are sad or anxious go underground (e.g., show up in behavior such as drinking too much) or are loaded into other emotions such as anger. Many domestic violence therapy groups help the men to identify other emotions beyond anger. For women, messages such as "you need a man to be happy," "girls don't do that" or "others are more important than you" fit in this category. Refer to the Brett and Rachel example in chapter 1 (pg. 6) to see these deeper emotional dynamics at work.

So how can we get a handle on this very powerful fight?

Fight #3 C's

Fight #3
C-Skills

- **Communicate Curiosity**
- **Cultivate Compassion**
- **Commit to Connection**
- **Advanced Skill: Create Rituals**

Fight Skill: Communicate Curiosity

Curiosity is a wonderful place to start. Rather than reacting to or offering advice to our partner when they respond with emotions, try being curious instead. I know this is very hard to do, particularly when a negative emotion is directed at you.

Try to ask questions when the pain comes close. Explore what your partner is expressing. *What size is the feeling? Besides being frustrated, what other emotions are there? How large is the sadness—more like a tennis ball or a large boulder? Do any images come to mind? A black hole? A shivering 4 year old? Does your partner have a previous memory of feeling this way? Who was around then? What event triggered the feeling?*

Sometimes people need help to begin to identify feeling words. The four most common are: MAD, SAD, GLAD & SCARED.[58] Behind expressions of anger are often the emotions of fear and sadness. Behind a person who shuts down during an interaction are often traumatic and competing emotions. It takes time to know yourself well enough to understand the powerful worlds within, particularly if you grew up in a family that was unsafe. Asking gentle questions is a good way to develop curiosity. Through curiosity you can better understand and attempt to care with more compassion.

Fight Skill: Cultivate Compassion

All persons share a deep need to be known and loved, particularly when showing our flaws and injuries. The word compassion means to feel with another (Com=With + Passion=Feeling). Compassion requires that we share an emotional space with another. When we demonstrate compassion, we connect to our partner. Our brain actually lights up when we mirror the emotions of another and when we attune to the feelings of another. We begin to create a safe place for our relationship to grow, heal and thrive.

A compassion example:

Ramon was a successful, college-educated businessman. His parents had immigrated to the US from the Dominican Republic when he was 7. He learned English quickly and his parents relied on him often to help them translate and understand their new world. Ramon married Susan, his college sweetheart, a few years after they graduated and after having been married for four years they had a 2 year-old son. Susan had requested that they come to therapy due to the increased arguments with her husband. Ramon had always been a driven man and this brought success to his business. However, at home, his intensity had become too much for Susan and she was fearful of the impact on their son. As we began to discuss their background, it became clear that Ramon had carried a huge burden for his parents as a young child, and that much of that burden had an underlying anxiety to it. Although unspoken, his parents fears regarding their immigration status and going back to their unsafe country was a large emotional burden for him. When Ramon worried about their son, his anxiety bubbled up as frustration and intense interactions with Susan. As Susan listened to this story of fear, tears came to her eyes; she gently held Ramon's hand and said, "that must have been so hard for a 7 year old." At this, Ramon became softer in the session and this continued in their relationship outside the therapy room.

When we cultivate compassion we also recognize that each person can be a gift to the other in the relationship. Each partner can become a healing agent in the life of the other. Maybe you did not sign up for this job description, but I believe this is central to partnering effectively within committed relationships.

Fight Skill: Commit to Connection

Most people long to feel securely connected to another and our biology actually validates this need. For example, our immune system functions best when we are in a relaxed and connected state within ourselves and with others. The current explosion of mindfulness practices indicates the power of being connected within.[59]

Research about couples confirms the power of being connected to others. On a behavioral level, successful couples respond to each other regularly each day in small but potent ways. *The Gottman Institute* terms this responsiveness between partners as *bids and turning*.[60] This happens when one person makes a *bid to connect* (e.g., scanning the room for your partner and then walking towards them) that is matched with *turning response* (e.g., the partner looks up and smiles). Couples who do not do this well can actually *bids and turning* to increase their commitment to connection.

However, actions are not the entire story. Attachment experiences also impact how the brain processes and influences the ways we make meaning of our world.[61, 62] When partners have a secure attachment in the couple relationship, each has an assurance that the other will respond. As you reach out, you know the other is there for you. Connected couples have confidence that their partner will respond when they phone or text with a need. Of course, this confidence is often severely challenged and distrust can prevail.

No partners connect perfectly all the time. Sometimes a fight happens because no connection has occurred. Missing each other can be an important reminder of the need for emotional intimacy and renewal. When couples attempt to repair the disconnection by asking forgiveness or restating the vows for connection, they can renew the relationship.[63]

Advanced Skill: Construct relational and personal rituals

For some couples, the intensity of past difficulties shows up very easily in the present. For these couples, it is very useful to co-create rituals of safety for the partnership and for both people to find ways to calm themselves.

I once did therapy with a couple who married later in life. They knew they needed to live in a space that allowed each of them to have a "cave" where they could retreat. Both had traumatic histories and both needed to be able to take a time-out when things got too intense. They had a term for this: *Cave Time*. When one of the partners would say this phrase, the other would nod. Both would "retreat" for 30 minutes and then they would come back together and give each other a hug. Fortunately, this couple was able to understand each other's needs. It is important that a couple negotiate a ***shared way*** to create a safe haven versus demanding that it look one particular way.

Strong feelings like fear and sadness motivate partners a lot in this third fight. We are bringing our more childlike and vulnerable parts into the relationship. It is hard work to do this fight well, yet it will be full of satisfaction and meaning when we do.

Fight #3 requires that we have room in our own life to carry another's struggles. Do you have room to take in another's pain? You have to keep your own tank full in order to keep going, which means that you will probably need more than your partner to fill your tank. You will need other social supports and ways to renew yourself. The next chapter aims to help you identify ways to do this.

EXERCISES FOR FIGHT #3

1. Identify several areas of "loss" that have been passed down to you.

2. Talk with your partner about a relationship in the past they had that "felt good" to them... (parent, sibling, friend, co-worker); then contrast this with a discussion of a relationship that "felt painful" to them. Have each person identify what were the most significant aspects of the encounters they had and the associated feeling (sad, valued, relaxed, angry, at peace, humiliated) that best describes what these were like for them.

3. Try out a "curious day" where you ask more questions and make fewer statements. Wonder how another is doing, another is thinking, or another is feeling. Follow up the first question with another question and then nod in response without a comment.

4. Develop some of your empathic abilities by sitting and breathing with another. Match them in their body posture for just a few moments. Wonder what their inner world is like. Take time to imagine what their day has been like before the two of you see each other.

5. Make this commitment for one day: each time your partner says something to you, make a conscious effort to respond to them, either by verbal exchange or by touch.

6. Identify an example of Fight #3.

Loading

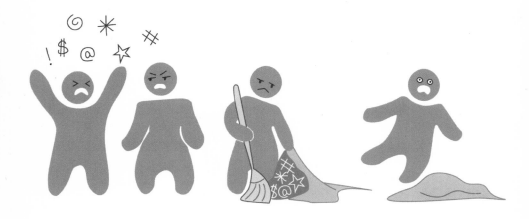

Coping

THE PERFECT STORM

or What Makes a Fight BIG

A BIG fight usually stems from two main things: **LOADING** and **COPING**.

At times, we are **loaded** with a combination of *all three fights*—individual differences (Fight #1), family/cultural backgrounds (Fight #2) and emotional baggage (Fight #3). In certain contexts, the three can intermix to create the perfect storm.

The other factor that can blow up a fight is **coping**. We can effectively or ineffectively manage our differences. Sometimes our actions lead to a positive outcome, but some add to the tension. We may cope by sweeping *the argument under the rug*. But when we ignore a fight, act as if it didn't happen and don't learn from a fight, it will trip us up later.

HOW MONEY CAN
LOAD A FIGHT

Fight #1 (Biology)

You fight since your partner said the cost of the jeans was about $100 when it was really $187.86. The amount is clearly over the budget and why can't you be more detailed??!!

Fight #2 (Family/Cultural Legacies)

Your partner reacts to your purchase of "expensive" concert tickets for your sister's birthday present. It's her 30th birthday and you wanted to make it special, an important tradition in your family.

Fight #3 (Relational Pain)

You've been working extra hours at a job you don't really enjoy, so you decide to meet some friends after work for an extra-long happy hour and you treat your friends too. After a few hours your partner calls; after some tense conversation, he begins yelling at you for not being home and for treating your friends better than him.

You think it's bad now? Loading and Vulnerable Timing

It may be a very BIG fight now, but be aware that fights often build up around significant life transitions. Having a child, moving to another state, getting married, losing a job, or dealing with aging parents are all times when fights load up. In all of these cases, each partner will deal with the transition a bit differently. Each will use what they have learned from their family or culture to navigate the transition and, often, there will be some unspoken emotional ties to the shift in life. Clients often seek out therapy during points of life cycle development, which makes sense since a convergence of competing agendas often dominate how they are trying to manage all that is going on.

The diagnosis of a severe or chronic illness can also add to the mix. Having dealt with many couples that must add illness as a partner into their families can add many practical, financial and emotional layers to the relationship. The build-up of stress over time can tip the scale into more conflict and a BIG fight.

A Few Tips for Managing a Loaded Fight

- When all three fights brew into one huge battle, slow down, breathe and take a time out.
- Give yourself permission to be confused.
- Identify that there are levels of intensity in your fights. Set up some sort of numbering system to rate the differences from smaller to larger intensity.
- Write down the date and time as well as associated words, feelings and things that you and your partner do in response to the BIG fight.
- If you can, begin to unpack the fight. Separate out Fight #1 from Fight #2 from Fight #3. For example, separate out how you needed to take some time out by yourself to

make sense of what was going on (Fight #1: you're more of an introvert), how the fight reminded you of how a family member would "deal with it alone" (Fight #2), and how the fight made you sad since your parents had divorced (Fight #3).

When Solutions Become The Problem

All persons cope with tensions in their lives. For example, you might limit daily conversation on your more progressive political leanings with your politically conservative partner. This may be helpful at times. However, not chatting with your partner about the different expectations that you and he have with your teenage son may become quite problematic.

Some coping strategies are productive and some are problematic and add another dimension to the original tension. Coping can either help you move toward each other and improve things or keep you more separate and stuck. This chapter lists instances where unproductive coping actually becomes the problem, followed by exercises to identify more productive coping.

Avoidance and Stonewalling

> As an overall coping mechanism, avoiding a fight can be associated with depression, anxiety, increased blood pressure and sleep problems[64] When we avoid the information we can gain from a fight, we cannot learn and grow. One key indicator of divorce is when a couple makes avoidance a pattern of relating.[65] Partners often experience withdrawl by their partner as abandonment, which reinforces the reactive pattern.

Triangulation

When you find it hard to talk with your partner, it is not unusual to find someone else to talk or complain to instead. While triangulation is a natural tendency to gain social support and understanding, it may not be productive. For many families, not dealing directly with the person that you have an issue with is a chronic pattern. People talk behind other's backs and don't value honesty, but pretend that all is well.

When hanging out with another is hanging out too long

Related to triangulation, infidelity can take several forms, sometimes physical, sometimes emotional and sometimes both. Deep connection between you and someone other than your partner can threaten your ability to stay intimate with your partner.

He's not drunk; he's just asleep on the couch (and other lies we tell ourselves)

Alcohol or substance abuse, and many other addictions, often start out as simple coping behaviors. Over time, they become a problem on their own. When pain exists in a relationship, addictive coping often becomes the way people try to numb the pain; addiction is a form of self-medication in which the medication becomes the focus of intimacy and not the partner.

Domestic violence

When people feel scared and helpless, they may resort to violence. Sadly, domestic violence is a huge and deadly problem in our society.

EXERCISES TO IDENTIFY PRODUCTIVE COPING

1. Write down some of your individual productive coping strategies (e.g., taking a walk, listening to music). List some of your partner's as well.

2. Write down some of your productive coping strategies as a couple (e.g., taking a time-out and coming back to the issue when you are both more calm).

3. Ask others to help you list some productive coping strategies (e.g., list times when you fought "better" as a couple and explore what was different than when you fought poorly).

4. Stop and reflect and find a word or phrase to describe what you were feeling when you had a fight with your partner. Identify what you needed and if you have told your partner about this.

5. Recognize your triggers before they have a hold on you; they are just beneath the surface. List some. When you are tired or hungry, you probably will not be as productive in your coping.

6. Review the battles you pick. Remember, you can win the battle and lose the relationship. Proving that you are right may not be the only way to win.

7. Meditate on the healing power of repair, reconciliation and learning afresh: apologize, forgive and let go—these can be amazing gifts to your partner and to you.

8. Note which Fight (#1 or #2 or #3) you are having most often. Try to use the skills associated with that particular fight.

MATCHING THE FIGHT

Fight	Description
#1 Different Biology	Making room for each "body", temperament, culture, personality and brain processing style
#2 Different Generational Legacies	Culture, gender roles, closeness and distance, values, rituals
#3 Different Relational Pain	Past injuries from traumatic and subtle pain, existential and spiritual coupling, intimacy built from empathy and compassion
The Perfect Storm	Elements of all three fights often during life transitions or a crisis like a medical diagnosis

TO THE SKILLS AND THERAPY

Skills	Type of Therapy
A-Skills: • Awareness with Acceptance • Add-to using Ands • Appreciation through Affirmation	• Strength-based • Focus on what is working • Acceptance and Appreciation • Shift to "WE"
B-Skills: • Be Patient • Become an Intentional Negotiator • Balance the WE, YOU and ME	• Gottman • Bowen • Transgenerational • PREP, Inc. • See page 124 and Reference 66
C-Skills: • Communicate Curiosity • Cultivate Compassion • Commit to Connection • Advanced Skill: Create Rituals	• Attachment • Emotionally Focused • Experiential • Trauma-oriented • Psychodynamic • See page 124 and Reference 66
• Slow down, breathe, take time out • Acknowledge confusion • Identify Intensity 1-10 • Write date and time and words, feelings and thing associated • Unpack the 3 fights	• Experienced Therapist

Don't Use a Saw to Fix an
Electrical Problem

HOW TO
Find the Right Professional Help

Start by Doing Your Own Homework

Sometimes you need to find a professional to help. For relational issues, you need to find a professional who works with couples. But first, it is helpful to get a clear sense of what is going on between you and your partner before you seek help from the outside.

If you want help with your relationship tensions and fights, my suggestion would be to take one fight theme at a time as described in this book and attempt some of the exercises at the end of each chapter, including an attempt to practice some of the skills connected to each fight.

Spending time with new information and new practices can help as you determine where you get particularly stuck. Use this book, other self-help books, and Internet resources to gain some guidance. You can't change overnight—it has taken awhile to get here, so give yourself some time and grace.

Two people go to the doctor complaining about chronic heartburn and indigestion. The first goes in focusing on the symptoms. The second reads some about chronic heartburn online, attempts to keep a two-week diary of food, times and indigestion reactions and brings this to the physician. The physician can probably help the second person more effectively since they have identified their particular issues and have begun self-help activities before seeking out a professional's services.

Steps to Find the Right Therapist for Your Type of Fight

All counselors are not created equal—I know. I have been training therapists, physicians and pastors for over 25 years. Some psychotherapists receive their license without ever conducting one hour of marital or couples counseling. Some lay counselors provide better counseling than those with a PhD. So where do you start to find good help?

The Foundational Step in Identifying a Good Couples Therapist

You may remember the old saying, if you're a hammer, everything looks like a nail. Each professional discipline uses language to make sense of problems along with their particular tools to fix them. If you own a Toyota, you want someone who works on Japanese cars to fix it.

Let's look at a couple that often fights about the topic of money. An accountant might see a couple's problem as a lack of developing a budget and keeping track of their spending on a balance sheet; a pastor might see the couple conflict as a spiritual issue that needs prayer and forgiveness; a medical doctor might offer medication to one of the partners who show signs of anxiety; a psychotherapist might offer communication skills training for the couple. All of these people may be wonderful professionals and may be helpful. So who's right? And how do you know whom to choose?

You will save time and money and get more expertise when you go to a therapist who specializes in working with couples.[66] Many therapists work mainly with individuals and not with couples.

It will benefit you to find a therapist who knows how to manage the particular needs of two persons seeking help together. A car mechanic cannot fix the battery without involving the operation of the engine.

The Second Step in Identifying a Good Couples Therapist

The second step is about you. While therapists or counselors share similar training and may have excellent general knowledge, consult a specialist who can offer expertise on your particular pattern. It would be helpful to identify what your needs are beforehand. For example, if you have a significant heart condition, wouldn't it make sense to go to a cardiologist (heart doctor) rather than a podiatrist (foot doctor)? Both can be excellent physicians, but one won't help you in the way you need.

A therapist can assist you better if you can identify the type of help you are seeking. It takes awareness and work to understand that you're in trouble and that your current coping is no longer working. The early chapters in this book are designed to help you identify the type or types of fights you are having. Can you begin to label where your relationship is getting stuck? What are the themes, emotions and behaviors tied to the tension-filled dance that has you and your partner stuck?

In my opinion, the best person to address **Fight #1** (different biology) is an experienced couple's therapist with a strength-based orientation. These therapists can manage and care about the tension of each person's frustration and can normalize the difficulties in becoming a WE. These therapists will also help the couple to identify how and when they are managing their inherent differences well; they don't just see the problems, they help you see the solutions you are already using. These therapists focus on acceptance and appreciation. Good therapists understand how tough it is to go through a developmental shift from being single to functioning as a unit; this shift takes time and commitment to new ways of doing things.

For **Fight #2** (different legacies), look for a couple's therapist trained in behavioral strategies and family or origin issues. Those using *Gottman* Method, *Bowen* Intergenerational Family Systems ideas and the PREP, Inc. relationship education program may be an excellent fit for this fight. Of the three fights, it will be easiest to find a good couple's therapist to help you with this one. The key is helping a couple communicate about their history and expectations, normalizing the differences that each person brings and negotiating potential new strategies and skills for working as a team through life.

Fight #3 (different relational pain) is the most emotionally taxing of the fights in my opinion, often touching on trauma issues and deeper psychological struggles each person brings to the relationship. Everyone has these, some more intense than others. Those clients who work with attachment ideas such as *Emotionally Focused Therapy* (EFT) can be an excellent match for this fight, as well as those who use other experiential, trauma-oriented and psychodynamic processes in their work with couples.

If you are struggling with **all three fights**, find an experienced couple's therapist who has many years of work under their belt and can work flexibly with the theories, techniques and approaches that will best support you.

The final step:

Review the therapist's website, read the *Informed Consent*, set up a "get-acquainted" session. Also, trust both of your gut instincts in weighing your choice.

Therapists throughout the nation are usually required by their state licensure or certification to have you sign an *Intake Form* and some sort of information about the services that they provide. You usually fill out and sign the intake form before meeting—this form is about you.

The *Informed Consent* is about your therapist—be sure to get this form and read it well. Often this information will be available on the therapist's website. It will include things like their education, their theoretical orientation, their experiences and training. You can ask the therapist to explain what these things mean in terms of the services and skills that they will bring into the room to help you. They will often list practical information about payment and times when they can set up an appointment to see you or get in touch with you. These practical things will also influence whether or not a "match" can work well.

When you find the one who appears to fit you best, set up a "get-acquainted" appointment. It's best if you both talk with the therapist on the phone or go in for an initial consultation. If you talk with the therapist briefly on the phone before you meet, pay attention to your reactions. Sometimes a therapist will meet with you for an entire session you will need to pay for; some therapists will give you an abbreviated time with no fee or a reduced fee.

After the basics of training, experience and practical issues, it's really about trust. Both partners need to experience the time with the therapist as one in which each felt heard and understood by the professional. Also, the therapist will be able to communicate a beginning summary of what is going on as well as some direction for the work you may do together. It is best to go into this initial session together. Be sure BOTH of you experience a fit, when only one does, to find another therapist that can be a better match for both of you.

A few questions to ask:
1. Do you work mainly with individuals or couples?
2. How long have you been in practice doing couples therapy?
3. What would couples say about your style of therapy?
4. Do you have a specialty?

The insurance dilemma: How to pay for help

Unfortunately, most psychotherapy services need at least one of the partners to evidence a "mental health diagnosis" (e.g., significant depression, anxiety) for medical insurance to pay for these services. However, sometimes a couple comes in with distress, but there is not a clear individual "mental health diagnosis." Without an individual diagnosis, you may have to pay for services out of pocket. Some Employee Assistance Programs will pay for a few counseling sessions as a part of your benefits; be sure to check with your Human Resources office to see if you have this type of coverage. Also, intern therapists or those early in their career may work for a lower fee.

Both you and the therapist can negotiate how often you will meet and for how long depending on how effective the therapy is in addressing your conflicts.

A little bit about couples therapy:

- The early part of therapy is called assessment and it includes gathering lots of information and identifying patterns.
- The therapist needs to facilitate an atmosphere of safety and fairness to both partners. However, not every session will feel balanced in terms of sharing or focus.
- Therapists are human too and can make mistakes and miss things; be sure to identify concerns you have along the way.
- Couples therapy will often stir up old hurts and memories. Remember that you need to address the infection in order to heal fully.
- Change takes time—most couples need to go to therapy for 10 or more sessions to see significant change.

Who should go in—the couple as a unit or the individual?

My first response is, anyone who is willing—a change in one person can have a very positive impact on the relationship; however, I strongly recommend that the COUPLE go in as a unit, at least for the first few sessions. The therapist benefits from experiencing and hearing from the relational (WE) and not just the individual partner's ME. Relationally-oriented therapists sometimes quote the famous adage: *The whole is more than the sum of its parts*. Remember the Myth buster chapter and the ME, YOU and WE of therapy? We need to talk about the WE, and both of you are vital in this conversation.

Individual therapy can help with the ME issue, but cannot address the WE of therapy very well. Having you both there is essential for relationally focused change experiences. Research suggests that individual therapy can readily lead more often to dissolving a relationship, while couple therapy leads more often to keeping the relationship intact.[67] If you want to make the relationship work, do the relationship work—together.

If you want to make the relationship work, do the relationship work—together.

GUIDELINES

Finding a therapist can be a daunting task. Having some guidelines for your search can help:

1. If you are open to this, ask friends, family, or other community members for recommendations.

2. Consider using your insurance. Sometimes your work will have an Employee Assistance Program that offers a few (about 3-5) free or reduced rate therapy sessions. You can also find out more about the psychotherapists that are covered by your insurance. Sometimes these therapists will have websites about the services they offer.

3. Do an Internet search using terms like "database for couples" or "marriage therapy." You will probably find several larger networks that you can then search using your zip code for professionals who work near where you live.[66]

4. Always review the individual provider's information on their website. Review the "About Me" or "My Approach" tab. You want someone who lists couples or marriage therapy on their information and training. Pay attention to your reaction when you read about this person as your potential therapist. If you find one you like, send the link to your partner to review also.

5. As a couple, go in for one "get-acquainted" session. It's worth the time, money and energy to begin with a good fit.

POSTSCRIPT

My husband told me about the short-story writer and poet, Raymond Carver, and his gravestone that overlooks the watery straights of Juan de Fuca in Port Angeles, Washington. Carver led a troubled life—filled with alcoholism, infidelity and bankruptcy. However, toward the end of his life, he was given a second chance through the love of a woman, Tess Gallagher. His epitaph is a poem carved into the black stone of his grave called, "Late Fragment." This poem is my encouragement to you.

And did you get what
you wanted from this life, even so?
I did.
And what did you want?
To call myself beloved, to feel myself
beloved on the earth.

REFERENCES
with Commentary

The following references can help you to better understand and explore the concepts and research noted in the book more fully.

1. The Gottman Institute (www.gottman.com) is a premier research center for our understanding of couple's relationships. Over three decades of observation and exploration have gone into their findings, studying both functional and dysfunctional couples interactions.

Gottman's research suggests that it is not conflict itself that is problematic, but rather specific characteristics of the interaction that couples have around the issues. In the study cited, for example, Gottman distinguishes between criticism versus complaint; criticism is related to a negative relational outcome while complaint is not. A criticism is judgmental of your partner, that he or she has a character defect. In contrast, a complaint is more specific and less personal. The important difference is in how a person verbalizes the problem. If seen as a character flaw, there are negative consequences; if seen as an "issue" that the couple must address, the conversation becomes more productive.

- Carrere, S., & Gottman, J.M (19990. Predicting Divorce among Newlyweds from the First Three Minutes of a Marital Conflict Discussion. Family Process 38(3), 293-301.

2. Several research groups identify patterns in couple relationships that tend to lead to divorce. In the PREPARE/ENRICH (www.prepare-enrich. com) research, couples that hold unrealistic expectations have a higher risk of divorce than those who have more realistic expectations. For example, some believe that romantic love will not change or fade, which is a common, yet untrue expectation. The Gottman Institute identifies particular couple interactions and physical responses that predict divorce.

3. Studies first developed by Dr. David Olson at The University of Minnesota (http://www.cehd.umn.edu/fsos/people/faculty/OlsonD.asp) use a Circumplex Model to describe the different patterns in a couple or family relationship. Research findings indicate that couples vary in their styles. PREPARE and FACES, assessment instruments that measure these differences, categorize couples into several categories including Harmonius, Vitalized, Traditional, Devitalized or Conflicted patterns. Other terms from different researchers such as in Emotionally Focused Therapy, define couples in Pursuer-Distancer and Blamer-Placater patterns. The Gottman Institute notes there are several couple patterns such as Conflict Avoiders and Validating types

4. PREPARE/ENRICH research suggests that the Traditional couple type may benefit the most from communication and conflict resolution skills. These marriages tend to rely on the partners having strong, congruent values that perhaps are not always spoken out loud. It follows that they would respond well to training that helps them talk about aspects of their marriage more skillfully.

- Fowers, B. J., Montel, K. H., & Olson, D. H. (1996). Predicting Marital Success For Premarital Couple Types Based On Prepare. Journal of Marital and Family Therapy, 22(1), 103-119.

5. According to The Gottman Institute, approximately 69% of the conflicts that couples have can be placed in a category called perpetual problems. By this they mean that a couple is negotiating something they can address but not fully resolve. For example, many couples have

a different level of need to socialize with others. As a result of this difference, it is very common for one partner to want to spend more time with people outside of their relationship. This difference will probably be evidenced throughout their relationship, will need to be negotiated regularly, and will not be completely resolved.

6. Both demanding and submissive styles of behavior in partners predicted poor marriage quality and depression in the relationship.

- Knobloch-Fedders, L. M., Critchfield, K. L., Boisson, T., Woods, N., Bitman, R., & Durbin, C. E. (2014). Depression, relationship quality, and couples' demand/withdraw and demand/submit sequential interactions. Journal of Counseling Psychology, 61(2), 264-279.

Depressive symptoms can be associated with the way a partner explains their spouse's behavior during conflict. It was particularly interesting that the findings were gendered, suggesting that some styles of interpreting marital conflict work better for men than for women and vice versa.

- Ellison, J. K., Kouros, C. D., Papp, L. M., & Cummings, E. M. (2016). Interplay between marital attributions and conflict behavior in predicting depressive symptoms. Journal of Family Psychology, 30(2), 286-295.

Affairs appear to have much less to do with sex than they do with particular interaction styles between partners. Recovery is hard work, but possible, after an affair.

- Brown, E. M. (1991). Patterns of infidelity and their treatment. New York, NY: Brunner/Mazel.
- Spring, J.A. (2012). After the Affair Healing the Pain and Rebuilding Trust When a Partner Has Been Unfaithful, 2nd Edition. William Morrow
- A couple's ability to engage in conflict while staying in touch with playfulness, enthusiasm, humor, and affection has the potential to affect the outcome of the relationship. These elements of fighting style are protective to the bond between partners.
- Driver, J. L., & Gottman, J. M. (2004). Daily Marital Interactions

and Positive Affect During Marital Conflict Among Newlywed Couples. Family Process, 43(3), 301-314.

7. When four particular characteristics and physical stress responses are seen during a brief couple's conversation, termed the Four Horsemen of the Apocalypse by The Gottman Institute, there is a very high probability that the couple will divorce. The Four Horsemen are verbal and non-verbal behaviors associated with contempt, criticism, stonewalling, and defensiveness.

8. Daniel Wile has done wonderful work to describe how couples repair their relationship after experiencing tension. Wile explains how a pursuer-distancer fighting style can be problematic in the marital relationship, and proposes how to arrive at a healthier style, which he calls engage-engage. Wile proposes that one important aspect of an engage-engage style is incorporating vulnerability and intimacy with each other by disclosing one's own feelings and longings instead of pointing the finger at the other person. This style allows the fight to become an opportunity for closeness.

- Wile, D. B. (2012). Opening the Circle of Pursuit and Distance. Family Process, 52(1), 19-32.

The Gottman Institute also studies couple repair attempts. Of particular interest were pre-emptive repair attempts found during the first three minutes of conflict. These behaviors helped establish a more positive trajectory for the entire fight.

- Gottman, J. M., Driver, J., & Tabares, A. (2015). Repair During Marital Conflict in Newlyweds: How Couples Move from Attack/Defend to Collaboration. Journal of Family Psychotherapy, 26(2), 85-108.

Specific repair actions seem to have the potential biological impacts. For example, a couple can lower their stress hormones (such as cortisol) more quickly during a fight by making brief statements such as saying "I'm trying to understand" or "I agree this is an important topic" or "I appreciate that you are trying to bring up this topic."

- Robles, T. F., Shaffer, V. A., Malarkey, W. B., Kiecolt-Glaser, J. K.

(2006). Positive behaviors during marital conflict: Influences on stress hormones. Journal of Social and Personal Relationships, 23(2), 305-325.

9. By using the metaphor of a fighting ring, I am not at all advocating physical violence as a way to deal effectively with differences. Anytime there is an abuse of power, physical or other, harm results. The statistics associated with domestic violence every year are staggering. For those who enjoy sports metaphors or sparring analogies, and can place themselves within this moving context between competent individuals, there may be merit in my use of this metaphor. However, I understand that some may be offended.

10. Second order change refers to the transitions needed to move to a new stage of development. In history we see an example of this in society's move from an earth-centered to a sun-centered explanation for the rotation of the planets—an entire system shifted. Second order changes are usually prompted when a person leaves or enters the family system. The shift is analogous to the movement of a hanging mobile when there is a rebalancing when something new is attached or removed from the mobile.

In families, for example, an enormous amount of reorganization must take place when partners become parents—a second order change. Each person, the couple relationship and the extended family/friendship/ work network need to shift in order to care for the new, vulnerable infant. Therapists see developmental stages as a time when huge psychological and social transitions are required; the same is true when people move from being a single adult to being a partnered adult.

11. Basic communication skills training can be extremely useful at times. Couple programs like PREP and Couple Communication include valuable skills. Many school districts include concepts from these basic social skills in their curriculum. I applaud these programs but also suggest that they are limited in effectiveness for some people.

https://www.prepinc.com/content/about-us/what-is-prep.htm
http://www.couplecommunication.com/

12. The amygdala is a part of the brain responsible for conducting rapid

yet crude appraisals of the environment, especially potentially dangerous situations. As such, the amygdala is responsible for our primitive fight-or-flight response.

- Preston, J., O'Neal, J. H., & Talaga, M. C. (2013). Handbook of clinical psychopharmacology for therapists. Oakland, CA: New Harbinger Publications.

The amygdala's capability for producing extremely fast reactions to environmental stressors is due to how there are several pathways of information that can travel to the amygdala.

- LeDoux, J. E. (1996). The emotional brain: The mysterious underpinnings of emotional life. New York: Simon & Schuster.

13. The Gottman Institute research suggests that the first years of marriage have a lot to do with negotiating couple differences while the later stage of marriage has a lot to do with maintaining the quality of the couple friendship.

14. Studies of brain imagery propose that some areas are related to particular personality traits. I have listed several of these studies.

- Ikeda, H., Ikeda, E., Shiozaki, K., & Hirayasu, Y. (2014). Association of the five-factor personality model with prefrontal activation during frontal lobe task performance using two-channel near-infrared spectroscopy. Psychiatry and Clinical Neurosciences, 68(10), 752-758.
- Modi, S., Rana, P., Kaur, P., Rani, N., & Khushu, S. (2014). Glutamate level in anterior cingulate predicts anxiety in healthy humans: A magnetic resonance spectroscopy study. Psychiatry Research: Neuroimaging, 224(1), 34-41.
- Rodrigo, A. H., Domenico, S. I., Graves, B., Lam, J., Ayaz, H., Bagby, R. M., & Ruocco, A. C. (2015). Linking trait-based phenotypes to prefrontal cortex activation during inhibitory control. Social Cognitive and Affective Neuroscience, 11(1), 55-65.

15. Some books on body clocks or circadian rhythms are listed below with a brief explanation.

- Baker, S.M., & Barr, K. (2000). The Circadian Prescription. New York: G.P. Putnam Sons. This book teaches how to tailor eating, sleeping, and other essential functions to our natural cycle or circadian rhythm. It claims this can positively affect your ability to achieve weight-loss goals, improve emotional balance, and feel energized.
- Edlund, M (2003). The Body clock advantage: Finding your best time of day to succeed in love, work, play, exercise. Avon, MA: Adams Media.

Edlund presents a practical approach using his "LENS" program, consisting of light exposure, exercise, naps, and socializing.

- Waterhouse, J.M. (2002). Keeping in time with your body clock. Oxford: Oxford University Press. This book gives advice on how to live in accordance with your body clock.

16. The findings of this literature review were mixed, but generally suggested that when a couple shared biorhythms they could coordinate activities together better which would benefit their marital relationship.

- Araoz, D. (1977). Biorhythm in couple counseling. American Journal of Family Therapy, 5(2), 34-39.
- Timmons, A.C., Margolin, G., & Saxbe, D.E. (2015) Supplemental Material for Physiological Linkage in Couples and its Implications for Individual and Interpersonal Functioning: A Literature Review. Journal of Family Psychology. 29(5): 720-731.

Couples reported higher marital satisfaction when they shared similar sleep patterns.

- Gunn, H.E., Troxel, W.M., Hall, M.Hl, Buysee, D.J. (2014). Interpersonal distress associated with sleep and arousal in insomnia and good sleepers. Journal of Psychosomatic Research. 76(3), 242.248.

17. The hormone, melatonin, is secreted from the pineal gland in the brain. One function of melatonin appears to tie to wake and sleep differences in people.

- National Sleep Foundation (2016). Sleep drive and your body clock. https://sleepfoundation.org/sleep-topics/sleep-drive-and-your-body-clock

This literature review of 19 studies found that while total melatonin production in a 24-hour period seems to stay the same as we age, for some it would lower.

- Scholtens, R.M., Munster, B.C., Kempen, M.F., & Rooij, S.E. (2016). Physiological melatonin levels in healthy older people: A systematic review. Journal of Psychosomatic Research, 86: 20-27.

This helpful webpage from Harvard Medical School gives examples of other factors that may disrupt sleep over the lifespan. For example, one partner may develop sleep apnea with age, which could dramatically change their sleep/wake cycles.

- Harvard Medical School. (2016). Changes in Sleep with Age. http://healthysleep.med.harvard.edu/healthy/science/variations/changes-in-sleep-with-age

18. These studies found that couples that did not share wake and sleep patterns had lower marital adjustment and higher marital conflict. However, within the mismatched group, if couples were able to be flexible and creative in their problem solving strategies, this was associated with better adjustment for the couple.

- Araoz, D. (1977). Biorhythm in couple counseling. American Journal of Family Therapy, 5(2), 34-39.
- Larson, J., Crane, D., & Smith, C. (1991). Morning and night couples: The effects of wake and sleep patterns on marital adjustment. Journal of Marital & Family Therapy, 17(1), 53-65.

19. The level of hormones does appear to impact the human sex drive and may be related to wake-sleep cycles as well.

- Hoffman, J.C. (1982). Biorhythms in human reproduction: The not so steady state. Signs 7(4), 829-844.

20. In this study, heterosexual couples reported actual and desired frequency of sexual contact. They also estimated their partner's desired frequency. Men's ideal frequency tended to be higher than women's, but both partners thought their partner's desired frequency was considerably different than it actually was.

- Simms, D., & Byers, E. (2009). Interpersonal perceptions of desired frequency of sexual behaviours. Canadian Journal of Human Sexuality, 18(1), 15-25.

21. These researchers measured the amount of eye contact 12-month old infants made with their parent, and found that female infants made significantly more eye contact than males. Furthermore, across sexes, 12-month old infants who had higher testosterone while in utero tended to make less eye contact. The authors of this study concluded that testosterone must play an important role in influencing social behavior.

- Lutchmaya, S., Baron-Cohen, S., Raggatt, P. (2002). Foetal testosterone and eye-contact in 12 month-old human infants. Infant Behavior and Development. 25(3), 327-335.

22. Newborn babies were studied to measure how long they looked at a face or a mobile. Male babies looked longer at the mobile, while female babies looked longer at a face. The researchers believe this suggests biological origins of sociability.

- Connellan, J., Baron-Cohen, S., Wheelwright, S., Batki, A., & Ahluwala, J. (2000). Sex differences in human neonatal social perception. Infant Behavior and Development. 23(1), 113-118.

23. Thee researchers present a review of the literature related to the effect of hormones in early development. Their inquiry implies that gonadal hormones, such as testosterone, influence some human behavior. Areas of particular relevance are childhood play behavior, aggression, and sexual orientation.

- Collaer, M.L. and Hines, M. (1995). Human behavioural sex differences: A role for gonadal hormones during early development? Psychological Bulletin 118(1): 55-77.
- Fischer-Shofty, M., Levkovitz, Y. Shamay-Tsoory, S.G. (2013).

Oxytocin facilitates accurate perception of competition in men and kinship in women. Social Cognitive and Affective Neuroscience, 8(3), 313-317.

24. According to the Diagnostic and Statistical Manual of Mental Disorders (DSM-5), premenstrual dysphoric disorder consists of various symptoms that appear only in the week preceding menses and the first few days of the menstrual cycle. These symptoms include (but are not limited to) strong emotions and mood swings, physical changes such as breast tenderness and lethargy.

There has been some controversy surrounding the addition of premenstrual dysphoric disorder (PDD) to the DSM-5. Some say that PDD being called a mental disorder represents unneeded negative labeling of a common lived experience (Browne, 2014). Other figures in the field of psychiatry argue that the body of research supporting PDD is insufficient to substantiate its addition to the DSM-5 (Offman & Kleinplatz, 2004). There is also research that suggests that PDD may not apply cross culturally. For example, in a study of Japanese women, the prevalence of PMS and PMDD (the equivalent to PDD at the time of the study) was much lower than that of American women (Takeda et al., 2006). No matter the direction the field of psychiatry takes with regards to PDD, PMS is certainly a salient cultural idea that comes up in clinical work with clients.

- Browne, T.K (2014). Is Premenstrual Dysphoric Disorder Really a Disorder? Journal of Bioethical Inquiry. 12(2), 313-330.
- Offman, A., & Kleinplatz, P.J. (2004). Does PMDD belong in the DSM? Challenging the medicalization of women's bodies. The Canadian Journal of Human Sexuality, 13(1), 17-27.
- Takeda, T., Tasaka, K., Sakata, M., & Murata, Y. (2006). Prevalence of premenstrual syndrome and premenstrual dysphoric disorder in Japanese women. Archives of Women's Mental Health 9(4), 209-212.

25. Brain studies using functional MRI technology note how individuals appear to perceive their environment a bit differently as noted on their scans. When given similar input, the brain appears to "light up" in different ways.

- Behler, O., von Ossietzky, C., Uppenkamp, S. (2016). The representation of level and loudness in the central auditory system for unilateral stimulation. NeuroImage 139, 176-188.
- Canli, T. (2002). Amygdala Response to Happy Faces as a Function of Extraversion. Science, 296(5576), 2191-2191.
- Filkowski, M.M., Olsen, R.M., Duda, B., Wanger, T.J., & Sabatinelli, D. (in press). Sex differences in emotional perception: Meta analysis of divergent activation. NeuroImage.
- Ford, J.H., Rubin, D.C., Giovanello, K.S. (2016). The effects of song familiarity and age on phenomenological characteristics and neural recruitment during autobiographical memory retrieval. Psychomusicology: Music, Mind, and Brain, 26(3), 199-210.
- Weiner, K. S., Jonas, J., Gomez, J., Maillard, L., Brissart, H., Hossu, G., Jacques, C., Loftus, D., Colnat-Coulbois, S., Stigliani, A., Barnett, M.A., Grill-Spector, K., & Rossion, B. (2016). The face-processing network is resilient to focal resection of human visual cortex. The Journal of Neuroscience, 36(32), 8425-8440.

26. Harvard developmental psychologist, Dr. Jerome Kagan, researched over many years to see how children's temperament is shaped both by nature and nurture.

- Kagan, J. (1997). Galen's Prophecy: Temperament in Human Nature. USA: Westview Press.
- Kagan, J. (2004). The Long Shadow of Temperament. United State of America: President and Fellows of Harvard College.
- Schwartz, C. E., Kunwar, P. S., Greve, D. N., Moran, L. R., Viner, J. C., Covino, J. M., Kagan, J.; S. Stewart, S. E.; Snidman, N. C.; Vangel, M. G.; Wallace, S. R. (2010). "Structural Differences in Adult Orbital and Ventromedial Prefrontal Cortex Predicted by Infant Temperament at 4 Months of Age". Archives of General Psychiatry. 67 (1): 78-84.

27. Although personality issues were not the only factors predictive of divorce in those who took this premarital inventory prior to marriage, it was one that was consistently influential.

- Fowers, B.J., Montel, K.H., & Olson, D.H. (1996). Predicting Marital Success For Premarital Couple Types Based on PREPARE Journal of Marital & Family Therapy, 22(1), 103-119.

28. How emotions are regulated varies with exposure to trauma. The brain is impacted by trauma events and, in turn, shapes how we process emotional information. Many current research projects are exploring this topic.

- Bonanno, G. A., & Burton, C. L. (2013). Regulatory flexibility: An individual differences perspective on coping and emotion regulation. Perspectives on Psychological Science, 8(6), 591-612.
- Fossati, A., Gratz, K. L., Somma, A., Maffei, C., & Borroni, S. (2016). The mediating role of emotion dysregulation in the relations between childhood trauma history and adult attachment and borderline personality disorder features: A study of Italian nonclinical participants. Journal of Personality Disorders, 30(5), 653-676.
- Nicholson, A. A., Rabellino, D., Densmore, M., Frewen, P.A., Paret, C., Kluetsch, R., Schmahl, C., Théberge, J., Neufeld, R.W. J., McKinnon, M. C., Reiss, J., Jetly, R., & Lanius, R. A. (2017). The neurobiology of emotion regulation in posttraumatic stress disorder: Amygdala downregulation via real-time fMFRI neurofeedback. Human Brain Mapping, 38(1), 541-560.
- Witting, A. B., Jensen, J., & Brown, M. (2016). Evaluating the utility of MFT models in the treatment of trauma: Implications for affect regulation. Contemporary Family Therapy: An International Journal, 38(3), 262-271.

29. This study found evidence suggesting that certain individuals had particular genes for dopamine receptors that are associated with novelty seeking and particular personality characteristics. Individuals high in novelty seeking have been described as emotional, impulsive, and exploratory.

- Ebstein, R.P., Novick, O., Umansky, R., Priel, B., Osher, Y., Blaine, D., Bennett, E.R., Nemanov, L., Katz, M., & Belmaker, R.H. (1996). Dopamine D4 receptor (D4DR) exon III polymorphism associated with the human personality trait of Novelty Seeking. Nature Genetics 12(1): 78–80.

30. This study compared the genetic markers (genotypes) related to serotonin processing in the brain. Different genotypes corresponded with higher or lower anxiety in the individuals studied.

- Murakami, F., Shimomura, T., Kotani, K., Ikawa, S., Nanba, E., & Adachi, K. (1999). Anxiety traits associated with polymorphism in the serotonin transporter gene regulatory region in the Japanese. Journal of Human Genetics, 44(1), 15-17.

31. Police detectives experience how different people report crimes and traffic accidents; researchers show some evidence of how the brain is involved.

- Gauthier, I., Skudlarski, P., Gore, J. C., & Anderson, A. W. (2000). Expertise for cars and birds recruits brain areas involved in face recognition. Nature Neuroscience, 3(2), 191-197.
- Krans, J., Näring, G., Speckens, A., & Becker, E.S. (2011). Eyewitness or earwitness: The role of mental imagery in intrusive development. International Journal of Cognitive Therapy, 4(2), 154-164.
- Bennett, P. J. (1986). Face Recall: A Police Perspective. Human Learning: Journal of Practical Research & Applications, 5(4), 197-202.

32. This comprehensive article outlines the various effects of stressors on an individual's health and the different factors and responses that affect the relationship between stress and health.

- Schneiderman, N., Ironson, G., & Siegel, S. D. (2005). Stress and health: Psychological, behavioral, and biological determinants. Annual Review of Clinical Psychology, 1, 607–628. Retrieved from http://doi.org/10.1146/annurev.clinpsy.1.102803.144141.

33. Some advocate that an evolutionary biology perspective can help us to understand gender differences.

- Geary, D.C. (2009). Male, Female: The evolution of human sex differences, Second edition. Washington, D.C.: American Psychological Association.

34. Genesis 1:27. So God created humankind in his own image, in the image of God he created them; male and female he created them.

35. It is foundational to start with acceptance versus pushing for change in this type of therapy.

- Jacobson, N.S., Christensen, A., Prince, S.E., Cordova, J. & Eldridge, K. (2000). Integrative Behavioral Couple Therapy: An Acceptance-Based Promising New Treatment for Couple Discord. Journal of Consulting and Clinical Psychology 68, 2, 351-355.

36. Homogamy refers to people who marry that share similar areas of life such as level of education, race and religion. Heterogamy refers to those who are different in these domains. People tend to connect with those who are more similar.

- Blackwell, D.L., & Lichter, D.T. (2000). Mate selection among married and cohabiting couples in US National Center for Health Statistics. Journal of Family Issues, 21(3), 275-302.

37. Henry Cloud and John Townsend's book on Boundaries is excellent.

- Cloud, H., & Townsend, J. (1992). Boundaries: When to Say Yes, How to Say No to Take Control of Your Life. Nashville, TN: Zondervan.

38. For an introductory look at the mind-skin connection and related specialties like psychodermatology or psychocutaneous medicine visit this online newsletter published from Harvard Health Publications of Harvard Medical School.

- http://www.health.harvard.edu/newsletter_article/Recognizing_the_mind-skin_connection

For a more scientific review of the field of psychodermatology, see

- Jafferany, M. (2007). Psychodermatology: A guide to understanding common psychocutaneous disorders. The Primary Care Companion to The Journal of Clinical Psychiatry, 9(3), 203-213.

39. For a comprehensive look at statistics regarding domestic violence in the United States visit the The National Coalition Against Domestic

Violence (http://ncadv.org/learn-more/statistics) where links to primary sources are included.

40. Roughgarden, Joan (2004). Evolution's Rainbow: Diversity, Gender, and Sexuality in Nature and People. Berkeley, CA: University of California Press.

41. This study examines the influence of gender on martial satisfaction and marital conflict. Findings discuss the influence of relationship factors such as gender roles, power, decision-making, conflict, flexibility, and well being. Results support the idea that gender roles influence marital satisfaction and marital conflict over time, especially that wives' perception of marriage predicts husbands' reported satisfaction and conflict.

- Faulkner, R., Davey, M., & Davey, A. (2005). Gender-Related Predictors of Change in Marital Satisfaction and Marital Conflict. American Journal of Family Therapy, 33(1), 61-83.

42. This study introduces an intervention that increases fathers' interaction with their babies and explores possible reasons for differential effects on areas of parenting.

- Doherty, W. J., Erickson, M. F., & LaRossa, R. (2006). An intervention to increase father involvement and skills with infants during the transition to parenthood. Journal of Family Psychology, 20(3), 438,447.

This thoughtful book, especially chapter 6, references the ways in which fathers and mothers attune and attend to their children depending on the child's gender.

- Pollack, W. (1999). Real boys: Rescuing our sons from the myths of boyhood. NY: Random House.

43. Husbands' continued labor force participation was predictive of decreased marital satisfaction for both husbands and wives. This finding could be linked to financial stress for couple or differences in gender roles, relationship equality, division of household responsibilities, and time together—not just husband working or not.

- Faulkner, R., Davey, M., & Davey, A. (2005). Gender-Related Predictors of Change in Marital Satisfaction and Marital Conflict. American Journal of Family Therapy, 33(1), 61-83.

44. Several researchers asked couples married for many years about the secret of enduring relationships. Key characteristics included intimacy balanced with autonomy, commitment, communication, religious orientation, and congruent perceptions of the relationship.

- Lampis, J. (2016). Does partners' differentiation of self predict dyadic adjustment?. Journal Of Family Therapy, 38(3), 303-318.
- Lee, J. E., Zarit, S. H., Rovine, M. J., Birditt, K., & Fingerman, K. L. (2016). The interdependence of relationships with adult children and spouses. Family Relations: An Interdisciplinary Journal of Applied Family Studies,
- Robinson, L. C. & Blanton, P. W. (1993). Marital Strengths in Enduring Marriages. Family Relations, 42(1), 38-45.

45. Ideas for Family Mission Statements

- Family Mission Statement [Online image]. (2016). Retrieved from http://momitforward.com/stregthening-family-creating-a-family-mission-statement/.
- Layne, E. (2015 May). Let Why Lead: Our Family Purpose Statement. Retrieved from http://letwhylead.com/2014/05/familys-purpose-statement.html
- Layne, E. (2015). How to craft a family purpose statement: A guide to discovering the "why" of your family and building an identity that will stay with your children forever [eBook].

46. Attitudes and practices of religion in a couple's relationship are associated with marital adjustment, perceived benefits from marriage, marital conflict, verbal collaboration, verbal aggression, and stalemates in disagreements for both wives and husbands. Religious differences add a significant dimension to the issues that a couple needs to address, particularly in relation to parenting.

- Crippen, C. & Brew, L. (2007). Intercultural parenting and the transcultural family: A literature review. The Family Journal, 15, 107-115.

47. Johnson, S. M. & Greenman, P. S. (2006). The path to a secure bond: emotionally focused couple therapy. Journal of Clinical Psychology, 62(5), 599-609. Quote is from page 599.

48. Perry, T. & Cannon, R. (Producers), & Grant, D. (Director). (2005). Diary of a mad black woman [Motion picture]. USA: Lionsgate.

49. Timberlake, J., Mosley, T., Harmon, J., & Fauntleroy, J. (2014). Not a bad thing. [Recorded by Justin Timberlake]. Larrabee Studios: RCA.

50. All people need to determine what is meaningful in their lives. We all struggle to make sense out of conflict and pain as well as joy and satisfaction. Often spiritual and existential questions are at stake. Couples often enter into this journey of making meaning together and can become agents of healing as they do.

- Docksai, R. (2012). Eight ways that longer lives will change us. Futurist 46(3), 20-23.
- Goodman, M.A., Dollahite, D.C., Marks, L.D., & Layton. (2013). Religious faith and transformational processes in marriage. Family Relations 62(5), p. 808-823
- Mahoney, A., Pargament, K. I. Jewell, T., Swank, A. B., Scott, E. Emery, E., Rye, M. (1999). Marriage and the spiritual realm: the role of proximal and distal religious constructs in marital functioning. Journal of Family Psychology, 13(3), 321-338

51. Individuals on the autism spectrum appear to have a lack of ability to mirror or understand the emotions of another. One area of research for this inability ties to the mirror neurons in the brain. Those with autism may have deficits in this area or "broken mirrors."

- Iacoboni, M. (2009). Imitation, Empathy, and Mirror Neurons. Annual Review of Psychology, 60.
- Ramachandran, V. S. & Oberman, L. M. (2006). Broken mirrors: A theory of autism. Scientific American, 17, 20-29. 52.
- Williams, J. H., Whiten, A., Suddendorf, T., & Perrett, D. I. (2001). Imitation, mirror neurons and autism. Neuroscience & Biobehavioral Reviews, 25(4), 287-295.

52. Chandler, L. (2015). The difference between empathy and compassion is everything [Blog post]. Retrieved from http://bigthink.com/ideafeed/compassion-is-an-action-not-an-emotion.

53. The costs of divorce on society and individual families are enormous. Work productivity, health problems, increased poverty and the negative impact on our children's legacy have been studied.

- Amato, P. R. & Keith, B. (1991). Parental divorce and the well being of children: A meta-analysis. Psychological Bulletin, 110(1), 26-46.
- Furstenberg, F. F. (1990). Divorce and the American family. Annual Review of Sociology, 16, 379-403.
- Holden, K. C. & Smock, P. J. (1991). The economic costs of marital dissolution: Why do women bear a disproportionate cost? Annual Review of Sociology, 17, 51-78.
- Kourlis, R. L. (2012). It is Just Good Business: The Case for Supporting Reform in Divorce Court. Family Court Review. 50(4). 549-557.
- Troxel, W. M. & Matthews, K. A. (2004). What are the costs of marital conflict and dissolution to children's physical health? Clinical Child and Family Psychology Review, 7(1), 29-57.

54. The National Healthy Marriage Resource Center http://www.healthymarriageinfo.org/index.aspx includes a variety of resources including state laws associated with premarital preparation programs. http://www.healthymarriageinfo.org/research-and-policy/other-resources/download.aspx?id=285

55. These studies asked couples to reflect on their marriage preparation program. Key areas they found useful included communication and conflict resolution training, the discussion of children and spirituality. They preferred programs that were active in couple activities versus lecture.

- Silliman, B. & Schumm, W. R. (2000). Marriage preparation programs: A literature review. The Family Journal, 8(2), 133-142.
- Williams, L. M., Riley, L. A., & Van Dyke, D. T. (1999). An empirical approach to designing marriage preparation programs. American Journal of Family Therapy, 27(3), 271-283.

56. Dr. Allan Schore's website lists his publications regarding relevant brain research, human relationships, and psychotherapy. http://www.allanschore.com/articles.php.

Healing Trauma, a book written by the lead researchers, clinicians, and theoreticians in the field of trauma and attachment, discusses both research and how therapy can help.

- Solomon, M. F. & Siegel, D. J. (2003). Healing trauma: Attachment, mind, body, and brain. NY: W. W. Norton & Company.

57. A podcast led by two doctors who discuss the relevance of research on brain plasticity for our everyday lives. The BrainHQ's SoundCloud page lists several podcasts related to brain research and includes more podcasts on neuroplasticity and healing.

- Merzenich, M. & Doidge, N. (2008, July) What is Brain Plasticity? Posit Science: BrainHQ Podcast. Podcast retrieved from http://www.brainhq.com/brain-resources/brain-plasticity/what-is-brain-plasticity or https://soundcloud.com/brainhq.

Also, Bonnie Badenoch's book, Being a Brain-Wise Therapist: A Practical Guide to Interpersonal Neurobiology (2008) is an approachable way to help you to understand brain science in our lives and relationships. It includes case examples and exercises.

58. Newer research from the Institute of Neuroscience and Psychology at the University of Glasgow published in Current Biology suggests the range of human emotion can be sifted down to four (not 6) basic emotions.

- Beck, J. (2014). The Atlantic. Retrieved from http://www.theatlantic.com/health/archive/ 2014/02/new-research-says-there-are-only-four-emotions/283560/.
- Jack, R. E., Garrod, O. G. B., & Schyns, P. G. (2014). Dynamic facial expressions of emotion transmit an evolving hierarchy of signals over time. Current Biology, 24(2), 187-192.

59. Many research articles support meditation and mindfulness practices to improve brain and immune function. Here are just a few.

- Davidson, R. J., Kabat-Zinn, J., Schumacher, J., Rosenkranz, M., Muller, D., Santorelli, S. F.,...Sheridan, J. F. (2003). Alterations in brain and immune function produced by mindfulness meditation. Psychosomatic Medicine, 65, 564-570.
- Greeson, J. M. (2009). Mindfulness Research Update: 2008. Complementary Health Practice Review, 14(1), 10-18.
- Keng, S., Smoski, M. J., & Robins, C. J. (2011). Effects of mindfulness on psychological health: A review of empirical studies. Clinical Psychology Review, 31(6), 1041-1056.

60. An introductory look at the Gottman research related to emotional bids and their implications in relational health.

- Lisitsa, E. (2012, Aug. 31). An introduction to emotional bids and trust. The Gottman Institute. Retrieved from https://www.gottman.com/blog/an-introduction-to-emotional-bids-and-trust/.
- Brittle, Z. (2015, April 1). Turn towards instead of away. The Gottman Institute. Retrieved from https://www.gottman.com/blog/turn-toward-instead-of-away/.
- Brittle, Z. (2014, Sep. 30). T is for turning. The Gottman Institute. Retrieved from https://www.gottman.com/blog/t-is-for-turning/.

61. Thoughtful work done by Dr. Dan Siegel explores the relevant research on interpersonal neurobiology, showing how the mind is influenced by your relationships and brain.

- Siegel, D. J. (2008). The neurobiology of "we": How relationships, the mind, and the brain interact to shape who we are [CD]. Louisville, CO: Sounds True, Inc.
- Siegel, D. J. (2012). The developing mind: How relationships and the brain interact to shape who we are (2nd ed.). NY: Guilford Press.

62. Emotionally focused therapy (EFT) is a type of couple's therapy useful for couples that want to find new ways to connect and experience each other.

- Johnson, S. M. (2008). Hold Me Tight: Seven Conversations for a Lifetime of Love. New York: Little, Brown & Company.
- Johnson, S. M. & Greenman, P. S. (2006). The path to a secure bond: emotionally focused couple therapy. Journal of Clinical Psychology, 62(5), 597-609.

63. Professor Worthington's website provides access to the findings of his research on forgiveness. The "Research" tab offers a list of articles to further explore regarding specific topics related to forgiveness.

- Worthington, E. (2016). How can you reach forgiveness? Retrieved from http://www.evworthington-forgiveness.com/.

64. A pattern of avoiding the discussion of important topics has many significant negative impacts on each partner and on their relationship. Sleep quality, depression and other factors of emotional health are discussed in these articles.

- Carmichael, C. L. & Reis, H. T. (2005). Attachment, sleep quality, and depressed affect. Health Psychology, 24(5), 526-531.
- Gottman, J. M. (1993). The roles of conflict engagement, escalation, and avoidance in marital interaction: A longitudinal view of five types of couples. Journal of Consulting and Clinical Psychology, 61(1), 6-15.
- Laurenceau, J., Troy, A. B., Carver, C. S. (2005). Two distinct emotional experiences in romantic relationships: Effects of perceptions regarding approach of intimacy and avoidance of conflict.

The Manage Conflict Part 1-4 blog posts talk about healthy and unhealthy approaches to conflict and how to identify which approaches you are taking and how to develop better ones in your relationship. Part 4 specifically talks about the physiological response and avoidance. Other blog posts at The Gottman Institute discuss stonewalling and how avoidance takes a physical and emotional toll.

- Brittle, Z. (2015). Manage Conflict: Part 1-4 [Blog post]. Gottman Institute. Retrieved from https://www.gottman.com/blog/category/column/new-construction/.

65. Review reference 7.

66. These websites allow couples to find workshops or a therapist in their area.

- The American Association for Marriage & Family Therapy
- https://www.aamft.org/iMIS15/AAMFT/Content/directories/locator_terms_of_use.aspx
- The Gottman Institute. (2016). Couples. https://www.gottman.com/couples/.
- American Bowen Academy. (2016). Find a Practitioner. https://www.americanbowen.academy/find-a-practitioner.
- The International Centre for Excellence in Emotionally Focused Therapy (2007). Find a therapist. http://www.iceeft.com/index.php/find-a-therapist.
- http://www.smartmarriages.com/app/Directory.BrowsePrograms
- The Doherty relationship institute. http://dohertyrelationshipinstitute.com/.

67. Doherty, W.J. (2002). How therapists harm marriages and what we can do about it. *Journal of Couple and Relationship Therapy, 1*, 1-17.

ACKNOWLEDGMENTS

To my husband, Larry—engaging dialogue companion, dedicated father and best friend: you have been my capable sparring partner and safe place. I appreciate that you have not given up your YOU while engaging with ME to create our WE.

To my adult children and their spouses—Jessica, Wes, Karis, Evan and Micah: you have encouraged my passions and shared me with lots of others. Thank you for bringing meaning and joy to my life.

To my Dad and Mom—Toby and Lucie, and to my extended family, Cyndi, LaNett, Megan, Caden, Deloris, Kathy, Gail, Dave, Jane, Marty, Greta, Clifford, Pascual and Cecile: your faithfulness through life is evidence of God's goodness.

To my skilled layout editor, Annie Mesaros, my creative illustrator, Suzi Spooner, my line editor, Madison Frambes and book cover designer, Rosie Gaynor: my gratitude for bringing my vision into a reality. You are all so talented.

To the many colleagues and family members who spent hours reviewing my early drafts, offering valuable feedback, doing research on my behalf and encouraging me—Suzi, Gerry, Taylor, Ryan, Stephanie, David, Jessica, Karis, Evan, Gail, Larry, Debbie, Jim, Lillian, Abby, Nolan and Jimmer—what a gift!

To my students and supervisees, particularly my graduate fellows: I have learned through and from you in so many ways—thank you.

To my clients who have trusted me during their struggles and allowed me to celebrate with them in their successes—you have been my teachers.

To my communities of support: the many companions in faith and professional friends in CFHA, SPU and AAMFT who have accepted me just the way I am and challenged me to become all I could be.

To my friends and colleagues—Tina, Gary, Stephanie, David, Peggy, Jeff, Hally, Doug, Jean, Scott, Hee-Sun, Don, Bill, Julie, Shawn, Michelle, Kurt, Tom, Monique, Steve, Lori, Michael, Kyleigh, Allison, Amanda, Kim, JoEllen, Todd, Larry, Lee and others—who hold places in my heart and my head: I cherish this journey with you and believe whole-heartedly that we are here to share our life purpose together.

ABOUT
the Author

Dr. Claudia Grauf-Grounds is a leading expert in Couple and Family Therapy, working for over three decades as a therapist, professor and supervisor. From the beginning of her career, she has specialized in couple's therapy. Besides doing therapy, Claudia advises and coaches graduate students to help them find their voice as therapists and equip them with the skills and confidence to launch their own careers. In 2007, she was recognized as Supervisor of the Year for the American Association for Marriage & Family Therapy—Washington Division.

Claudia is a tenured professor of Marriage and Family Therapy at Seattle Pacific University in Seattle, Washington and co-author of ***Essential Skills in Family Therapy***, a primary textbook for family therapists as well as many professional articles.

Besides practicing as a licensed marriage and family therapist in Washington State and California, she has taught and supervised graduate students at the University of San Diego, Rosemead Graduate School of Psychology as well as Bethel and Seattle Pacific Seminaries. She held Clinical Faculty positions training primary care physicians through SHARP Heathcare in San Diego and the University of Washington School of Medicine. She presents nationally and internationally on couples, families and relational systems ideas, supervision and medical family therapy.

Dr. Grauf-Grounds grew up in San Diego, California. She completed a BA in psychology from Stanford University as well as receiving honors in humanities. She met her future husband, Larry, a Presbyterian pastor, while playing intramural flag football together at Fuller Theological Seminary. She completed her masters in theology and counseling at Fuller and then her PhD in sociology and family therapy at the University of Southern California. She is the mother of three grown children (who are all amazing). She resides in Seattle where she loves to watch movies, throw dinner parties and remodel homes.